STUDIES IN INTERNATIONAL SECURITY

*

STUDIES IN INTERNATIONAL SECURITY: 4

WORLD ORDER AND NEW STATES

PROBLEMS OF KEEPING THE PEACE

Peter Calvocoressi

With a Foreword by

Donald Tyerman

FREDERICK A. PRAEGER

Publisher

NEW YORK

FOR

THE INSTITUTE FOR STRATEGIC STUDIES

LONDON

BOOKS THAT MATTER

Published in the United States of America in 1962
by Frederick A. Praeger, Inc., Publisher
64 University Place, New York 3, N.Y.

© The Institute for Strategic Studies 1962
Library of Congress Catalog Card Number: 62-16841

Printed in Great Britain

CONTENTS

Foreword

by Donald Tyerman

ONE of the prime needs of an age of intersecting revolutions —military, political, economic—in which the problems of maintaining peace and international order inevitably become more complex, is to develop a means of communication between the expert and the thoughtful citizen. It is to this need that the Institute's series of studies is addressed. They are intended, not as major contributions of independent research, but rather to lay out the map of a particular problem in international security so that scholars and lay men alike may have a foundation on which to develop their own researches and conclusions.

We who are associated with the work of the Institute are particularly grateful to Peter Calvocoressi for undertaking, in the course of a busy life, this analysis of a problem that has hardly been explored at all—the instability created by the rise of a great many new sovereign states at a time when the great powers have lost their old freedom of action against the spread of disorder, but before the new peace-keeping machinery of the United Nations has acquired either the capacity or the acceptance to serve instead. There were few precepts and precedents to guide him. The lucid, elegant, and sometimes eloquent statement of the problem in these pages is the result both of his own clear and balanced thought and of access to the experience of many different kinds of people, national and international Civil Servants, soldiers and police officials, politicians, travellers and writers.

This book represents Mr. Calvocoressi's own deductions from the evidence and the conclusions are, of course, his own. He was assisted by a study group which met regularly at the Institute during the first seven months of 1961 under my chairmanship. Its members were: General Sir Geoffrey Bourne; Andrew Boyd; Brian Crozier; Geoffrey Goodwin; Joseph Harsch (U.S.A.); Michael Howard; Charles Janson; James Lemkin; Malcolm

Mackintosh; Commander H. Mulleneux; Edouard Sablier (France); Brigadier W. F. K. Thompson; Mrs. Shirley Williams; Colonel A. E. Young; Maurice Zinkin. The study was then used as the working document at the Institute's Third Annual Conference at Geneva, where its conclusions were commented upon by over one hundred people from seventeen countries, representing a wide range of opinion and experience. Our special thanks are due to a number of busy officials who contributed their own insights and experience to our discussions.

Finally, we have to thank the Rockefeller Foundation for making a grant to Mr. Calvocoressi, without which it would have been impossible to initiate this study.

Author's Foreword

THE territory into which I have ventured in this study is, though not unknown, yet largely unmapped. We must therefore expect to stumble and not mind doing so, to start off along false trails, to experience bafflement and sometimes a wild hope. When Mr. Alastair Buchan invited me to do this work I was prudent enough to hesitate, but not prudent enough to refuse, for I found the prospect exciting. I hope that in the upshot I may have opened arguments that others will be able to follow and extend. I do not claim to have done more.

I have received much help. The discussions of the study group assembled by the Institute brought together general propositions, particular illustrations, and practical experience. The arguments we had and the facts adduced by members of the group have been very valuable. The three days of debate at Professor Freymont's Institute at Geneva added, corrected and above all helped me to formulate the setting in which these problems have to be seen and solved. Mr. Buchan himself has been the best sort of critic, encouraging but sharp, and—by no means his least contribution—so obviously caring about these things. I am also indebted to a number of friends who have helped me to give point and precision to what I have written: particularly, among those whom I may name, to Mr. Richard Harris and Mr. Guy Wint. And I owe special thanks to Mr. Maurice Keens-Soper, who both prepared and chronicled the meetings of the study group and pursued a variety of trails with diligence, intelligence, and effect.

P.C.

Aspley Guise,
November 1961

Chapter *1*

The Setting

THERE exists today a valid fear of disastrous war and therefore an urgent need to prevent it. These propositions seem to me self-evident and to justify therefore every attempt to analyse the roots and branches of our present disorders and to suggest ways in which sensible men may face insensate forces. If you ask the first person you meet in the street why peace seems particularly precarious, his answer will most likely include some reference to nuclear bombs and missiles. The availability of unlimited force is certainly as terrifying as it is new, but it transforms the consequences of conflict rather than the sources. The existence of force is not by itself a threat to peace. The use of force is indeed the normal way to keep the peace. Men (with the possible but not very pertinent exception of Eskimos) quarrel and come to blows. Where they are few and remote their affrays concern nobody but themselves, but where they are many or at hand their fellows may feel prompted to prevent or interrupt their quarrels lest they spread and do damage. In some times and places men have been restrained by remote control, literally by the fear of God, but even the Truce of God had to be imposed by human authority and backed by human force to make sure that it worked. All over the world authorities use force to keep order and are commonly judged by their success or failure in this very function. An authority which allows breaches of the peace is thought to have betrayed its *raison d'être*; faced with an upheaval it will announce that its first duty is to restore law and order, meaning that it intends to call out troops and expects to be commended for doing so.

Only the smallest of societies enjoy peace by consent and without coercion. In most a degree of force is essential. It may be truer, and it sounds more agreeable, to say that peace rests on power than to say that it rests on force, which is only one ingredient in power. The distinction verges on the semantic, but it is valid subject to the considerable and debilitating proviso that the other ingredients are, even cumulatively, comparatively ineffective. If peace rests on power, it is nevertheless true that power in this context means force nine-tenths of the time, so that without force you cannot be sure of having peace and it is illusory to suppose anything else. One may, and should, deplore this state of affairs and continually remind others of its inadequacies and work to improve it, but equally one may not gloss over it or imagine that it is likely to change substantially within a matter of centuries. One day, perhaps, international society will enjoy peace by forbearance. At present, it needs compulsion as well and most of the time, for in politics there is no authority unbacked by force.

But the man in the street who fears nuclear weapons is right all the same. Although force, even annihilating force, may be a necessary part of world order, conflicts of force may destroy that order and mankind, too. The precariousness of peace is a consequence of a coincidence—the arrival of unlimited force at a time when it is more likely to be used in the service of sectional antagonisms than as an auxiliary of a universal police. Have we more than we can cope with when we are required to handle at one and the same time weapons of mass destruction, an acute schism within our own civilization, and the huge difficulty of creating understanding and amity between our Western society and other peoples, ancient in civilization but many of them new to statehood, whom the West so recently dominated? Nuclear power appals because of its potential use in barely controllable conflicts. Unless we can resolve what we call the East-West conflict (meaning the conflict between the eastern and western wings of Western civilization) and the vaguer encounters between European, Asian and African civilizations, peace is not established and nuclear war is always round this corner or the next. History has played a trick on us by landing us in this crucial position and that is why we need to take a look at the historical setting before examining the present or groping towards the future.

The Western tradition is a dual one. It is, first, a moral tradition established by teachers stretching from Socrates and Sophocles to Dante. It is a tradition which extols justice and *philia* (love of your neighbour) and insists upon the supreme value of the individual conscience. These are the things it sanctifies; it does not sanctify peace; indeed, justice and conscience are rebellious rather than conservative, disturbing rather than placatory. The heroes and heroines of the tradition, from Antigone onwards, have all been rebels and most of them have been ready to shed blood at the call of righteous indignation which, agreeing with Blake, they identify with the voice of God. This tradition was reinforced by Christianity, which is one of the less pacific religions, and was then revivified about five hundred years ago by the renaissance of classical humanism and the Protestant Reformation's initial appeal to conscience against authority.

But the Western tradition contains also a second strand, no less powerful and in some sense contradictory. This is respect for law, the legacy of the Romans, although it too owes something to the Greeks by way of the Stoics. This respect for law is essentially conservative and pacific (as can most clearly be seen in its extreme and caricatured form of a love of order *per se*). The Romans endowed the idea with practical apparatus by creating the Civil Service and the roads without which authority in the form of the State cannot function. They made centripetalism a doctrine of political faith, and so long as they were strong enough to have their way, they ensured much peace over a large area. They also gave the European mind a new cast which it could not have derived from the anxieties of a moral tradition, for their assured and practical orderliness contributed to the formation of what we now call a scientific way of thought, and thus to the great scientific advances of the seventeenth century which set Western civilization ahead of its rivals and gave Europe a temporary domination over much of the world, as astonishing as Rome's own imperium at the beginning of the Christian era. This Roman strand survived the dissolution of the western Roman empire thanks to the Roman Catholic Church and, after the political failures of successive western empires and of the papacy, found fresh embodiment in the

states established by the Normans in southern and north-
western Europe and by their imitators. These states, and not
the empires which laid claim to the Roman name, are the true
successors of the Roman state, and the system which formed
around them lasted in Europe down to our time. This state
system is now in flux, perhaps in decay. It did not keep the
peace efficiently, but it carried on its back, like Arion's dolphin
bound for a new shore, the notion of the rule of law, and if the
West is to be true to its tradition it has to retain this notion in
its own changing structure and also to try to apply it in the
world at large.

Unfortunately the structure of Western society is strained not
merely by a shift away from the familiar state system in Europe
to something still not clearly perceived, but also by an ideological quarrel which is in some eyes tantamount to a disintegration of Western civilization itself. This quarrel has consequences
which bear forcefully on the subject of this study.

The Bolshevik revolution in Russia was not the first occasion
on which an upheaval in one European country has been accompanied by a deliberate attempt to create parallel upheavals
in other countries and to subvert an order as well as change a
government. The French revolution had the same aim and
used war for this purpose. Between the wars for the *limites
naturelles* and the imperialist wars of Napoleon there was for a
short time a revolutionary belligerence devoted to making
Europe quite a different place. The directly subversive impact of the French revolution was shortlived, that of the
Russian revolution has persisted.

There is a belief that there exists in Moscow a master plan
for the subjugation of the world by a date in the foreseeable
future. I do not share this belief, for which I know of no evidence
and which seems to me inherently improbable. But, assuming
my disbelief to be well founded, it does not follow that the Communist doctrines of the Russian revolution must be accounted
to have ceased to have an influence on world affairs, for even if
there is no Communist grand design there are Communist preconceptions which, whether obsessively or unobtrusively, condition the thoughts and policies of Russian—and Chinese—

statesmen. This Communist groundwork gives to Russian impulses a character different from the interventions of Western powers in international affairs, for Communists have inherited from their forebears and indeed still learn for themselves a missionary zeal, a capacity for organizing revolution, and an attitude to peace as a sort of refined war, a war without overt physical onslaughts. The world beyond the Communist borders becomes for them an area of conflict where the word peace defines the kind of struggle that is being waged and does not connote the absence of strife. Thus Russian policy has, for ideological reasons, no vested interest in world order.[1] Further, it does not recognize the legitimacy of the existing order, which Western statesmen seek to maintain even though they may also wish to make changes in it.

It is, therefore, mistaken to assume that the Russian and American impacts in world affairs are alike. This mistake springs, I believe, from a circumstance which is something of a novelty in international affairs. The fears that beset so many people when they think about the state of the world are not fears of the United States. They are not even primarily fears of the U.S.S.R. They are fears about the relations between these two giant powers. Whereas in the past a smaller country has usually feared first and foremost a greater neighbour, now the dominant fear focuses on a pair and not upon a unit. Hence it is easy to treat the two members of the pair as equally to blame for the stresses and strains of everyday international life; the sufferers ignore the different aims and motives of the protagonists and interpret their equivalent power and hostility as equal menace to everybody else.

These fundamental differences import also differences in opportunity and method. The U.S.S.R. has not only a special impulse to change things in various parts of the world but also special advantages in pursuing this object. It has the advantage of central control, since other Communist parties are with few exceptions willing to take orders from Moscow, and this control confers on Moscow the further advantage of being able to

[1] For national reasons it has no vested interest in the existing order in certain areas, e.g. Persia.

choose its own timing. (The rise of Peking and the independence of Belgrade have curtailed these advantages and will do so further.) Then Moscow has also the advantage of secrecy, since it can use small groups of local residents to make mischief, whereas Washington commands no such units and would probably not be able to use them if it did; the West exerts influence through majorities, but the Communists can do quite well through minorities. Finally, the Russians have perfected the weapon of subversion which, more than anything else, has baffled political strategists on the other side.

Subversion—the clandestine attempt to undermine a régime or a society beyond one's own borders—is not new, but the Russians have perfected and expanded it; the Russian word *provokatsia* embraces not merely the exploitation of a situation for subversive ends but also the deliberate fabrication of the situation. Thus the Russians have added to their armoury a new tool which enables them to intervene in areas thousands of miles away from the Soviet army's beat. They have been assisted in two ways. First, given their attitude to international society, they see nothing wrong in subversion, since that which is to be subverted has no legitimacy in their eyes; the West, on the other hand, has some inhibitions (which should not be exaggerated and clearly have not been of great weight in the U.S. Central Intelligence Agency any more than they used to be with the British when they found silver as useful as lead in their less overt dealings in distant parts) against adopting underhand methods to remove governments with which relations are formally correct. Secondly, the enormous speed of social change in many parts of the world presents would-be subverters with opportunities that are many and fruitful. Although subversion is a technique exploited by Communits for Communist ends, the occasion for applying it need have nothing to do with Communism. Any malaise will do. Thus the friction in India over languages, though completely divorced from any question of social or political ideology, provided Communists with opportunities simply because the Indian Government's refusal to accept all the recommendations of its own commission gave rise to local irritation; in Bombay serious riots ensued and the Communists joined in something which they could not themselves have started. Such riots need not lead to a world war or even to a local war, but they constitute breaches of the peace and in states where democratic institutions are weak these institutions are themselves endangered. New states are, moreover, usually weak in their security services, so that they are unlikely to know what is happening until it is too late. At the time of the Indian language riots the Chief Minister of the Punjab promptly put all available trouble-makers in jail, thus avoiding the disorders which beset Bombay, but in another place at another time authority will be slower to react, disorder will erupt and spread, and the area of conflict may eventually become so large as to threaten more than local law and order.

Where Communist doctrines appeal or Communist methods beguile anti-Communists are inclined to feel helpless. In the nature of things they can neither stop subversion nor do it back with much success, and in most cases they are reduced to complaining that it is all very unfair. The essence of their complaint and their impotence lies in the secrecy of the tactics which they deplore, and once this is grasped their correct counter-moves should become obvious: they should anticipate the Day of Wrath with its promise that the hidden shall be made plain and the transgressor overtaken by retribution. Their first task is to bring what they dislike into the open and spread an awareness of proceedings which, in their belief, have only to be exposed to be resented and frustrated. The weakness of subversion as a weapon is the implication that if you resort to secret means you must be up to no good. The fact that Communists work in this way is potentially a boon to anti-Communist propagandists who are seeking to persuade the uncommitted that the prime and sinister aim of Communist policies is to gain control of other people's destinies. Mr. Nehru, who is the outstandingly successful practitioner of the art of keeping on good official terms with the U.S.S.R. while dishing his own Communists, adopted long ago a policy of deflation and vaccination. He treats Communism as something rather old-fashioned which can be of no possible interest to the young, and he encourages Indians to go to Moscow and see what the U.S.S.R. is like.[1] The importance of Mr. Nehru's example lies in its demonstration of how to conduct political warfare, even in a novel and peculiarly baffling field, without leading to a recourse to arms. The West's second task in relation to subversion is to divorce these Communist activities from nationalism, for subversion has had few successes where it has not been allied with an anti-Western nationalism—a subject to which we will revert in the last chapter.

If the impact of the U.S.S.R. in international affairs is as I have described it, how far is it a threat to peace? Peace is a word which it is easy to quibble about. In a sense we have no peace and we are not trying to keep the peace, because we cannot keep what we do not already have; we are trying to win or establish or create peace. There is a conflict in the world which is at once a conflict between two giant powers and a conflict between two ideas of what the world ought to be, and this dual conflict goes on all the time and is not likely to end at all soon. We wish to bring this conflict to an end, however gradually, but we are also concerned to prevent it from getting worse and producing universal violent war. Such a war could begin in one of three ways. It could begin as a direct trial of strength between the United States and the U.S.S.R., for example in Berlin or in Persia. It is safe to assume that nobody wants this to happen, but it is not so safe to assume that it will not. It is true that a clash of this kind has so far always been avoided, for example in Laos, but it is not justifiable to assume that it will be avoided next time. This study is not directly concerned with these possibilities, although the reader needs to have them in mind when considering the two other possible sources of violent war, which constitute the core of the chapters which follow.

Besides a great war begun by great powers there is danger of war from a local conflict between two lesser powers or from local disorder arising within a single state. The commonest cause of a war of the first kind is a territorial dispute. Europe has by now resolved or suppressed most of its purely irredentist

[1] Anti-Communist students are fabricated in Moscow, Communist ones in British and French universities.

problems, though the division of Germany entails a danger of war which has irredentist as well as other components. But outside Europe the removal of Spanish colonial rule engendered frontier disputes throughout South and Central America which a century and more of independence has not cured, and similar problems are now arising in other continents in the wake of other retreating colonial powers. Even if these colonial powers had ruled territories delimited by nature or race or tongue, the dislocations of independence could hardly have failed to strain the map, but since the old frontiers were in many cases arbitrary, unnatural, and even absurd, they cannot be expected to remain unaltered, and it would be optimistic indeed to suppose that the alterations will always be peaceful. In addition many of these new states are multi-racial, and if their races cannot learn to live side by side, they will have little internal order and will be a menace to more than themselves.

Since new states are many, the occasions for trouble of this sort are many too. Although some of them may be settled without fighting or with no worse than local wars, the worldwide interests of the giant powers give all local conflicts a wider potential. Each great power is likely to sympathize with and support one party or the other, and if the two parties go to war it may be difficult for their patrons to keep out. Similarly an internal local conflict (which is no more than a conflict between two people in the same house as opposed to a conflict between neighbours) may embroil major powers in the same way. Thus the instability and border disputes of new states (as of other lesser powers) constitute a threat to world order because of the temptation for greater powers to interfere. These major powers may abstain through fear of the consequences to themselves of intervention in a particular place, but there is little sign of their forbearing to intervene by agreement, even by tacit agreement. If, moreover, they do hold off, there remains the problem of resolving the local conflict by persuasion or compulsion instead of letting it grow until the major powers are overwhelmingly tempted to intervene or positively begged to do so.

We shall in what follows examine first the threat to peace from local conflicts of the one kind or the other, across or within frontiers, and the attitudes of major powers to conflicts of this sort—what factors make for their intervention, what inhibitions restrain them. If at this point we conclude that there is no reason to suppose that the great powers are likely to keep the peace of the world any better in the future than they have kept it in the past, we need to consider what may be done to give us a better chance of avoiding major wars; and we shall in particular inquire into ways of rectifying the alarming instability of new states, and of acting through the United Nations to prevent or contain disorders that seem likely to burst the bounds of local control.

Chapter 2

The Limitations of Major States

THIS study is concerned with keeping states at peace among themselves and with avoiding the grosser kinds of civil strife within states. For some time past the state has been the accepted and dominant unit in international politics, rather like the political party in a democracy. It is therefore logical to begin by considering the contributions, pacificatory or otherwise, which states may make to our problem, and it is convenient to draw a large distinction between states that are older, more firmly established and on the whole more powerful and on the other hand the newer states which are usually poorer and weaker (though not necessarily without resources and prospects). States in the senior group are able to contribute to peacekeeping by example, by experience, and above all by compulsion, but the complexity of their interests and their motives, together with the limitations which they weave about one another diplomatically and strategically, make them at best part-time and half-hearted guardians of the peace: they have so many other things on their minds. In this chapter I wish to analyse first the kinds of disorder that have characterized the upheaveals of the post-war years, secondly the forms of intervention available to the larger states anxious to limit these disorders, and finally the factors which impel these states to act as policemen and those which disincline them from this role and make them prefer to hold back.

The record of disorder since the end of the Second World War is a full one. The rollcall is so long that one hesitates to recite it. About half the states in the world and far more than half the non-sovereign dependent territories have experienced violence in some degree. The largest category of upheaval is that which may be labelled the protest against colonialism, and the troubles comprised in it are akin to the risings in nineteenth-century Europe which were a liberal and nationalist protest against the alien and imperial rule of Austrians, Russian and Ottoman Turks. Madagascar, Indonesia, Indo-China, Kenya, Nyasaland, Algeria, Cyprus—these are the more obvious cases from the annals of the decline of Europe overseas. Hungary and Poland have shown that Europe itself has not yet shed this source of pain and grief and may indeed be left with it after Asia and Africa find that there are no more colonial pricks to kick against—unless, as Tibet, Vietnam, Laos may demonstrate, a new colonialism re-orients old grievances and so keeps them alive. Moreover, the process of decolonization creates stresses in the retreating as well as the emerging states, as the post-war history of France sufficiently attests.

A second major source of post-war disorder is internal conflict, whether arising from race or religion or unjust government: communal and language riots in India and the fragmentation of Burma after independence, the wholesale but still incomplete dismantling of *anciens régimes* in the Middle East, the movement throughout Latin America of which the Perons used to be and Fidel Castro now is the best known exemplar, the rumblings of change in Ethiopia, the tyranny of the Afrikaner minority in the Union of South Africa. Nor, once more, is Europe exempt from these ills. France came within an inch of civil war in 1958 and 1961, and Spain and Portugal could do the same at any time without causing any great surprise. In the late 'forties both France and Italy were regarded as likely battle-grounds for Communists and anti-Communists, while Greece's archaic society and economy were only saved from Communism by military intervention by Western states. The whole of the Mediterranean litoral (except only southern France, Northern Italy, and possibly Lebanon and Israel) is a depressed area inhabited by peoples who are not only poor but can compare their poverty with the better fortunes of others not far away and so have discovered that they need not be so poor. Their material distress and inevitable indignation make them ripe for an ideological takeover bid, for it stands to reason that anybody with a system that promises better things is certain to gain a hearing. But however disagreeable and reprehensible these sources of internal conflict, it has to be said that they are not necessarily a threat to peace on a wide scale. Where disorder is quickly dealt with, the threat evaporates. Only where forces are evenly balanced and the conflict long, as in the Spanish civil war, does the rest of the world have to take cognizance and perhaps action.

Next there is a third and allied category of inadequacy. Disorder has occurred where it need not have occurred, but for the incompetence of government. We have seen breakdowns of law and order, actual or imminent, in Pakistan, the Sudan, Lebanon, and Turkey, but the prime example is, of course, the Congo, where a new state, having been hustled into existence without the necessary civil apparatus, was found after ten days to have been deprived also of its ultimate source of authority, the army, which had disintegrated through bribery and become the basis for an anarchic warlordism. Government was rendered ineffective or non-existent; civil war supervened; and, rightly or exaggeratedly, even world war seemed a possibility. The history of independent Indonesia is a further example of the hazards of weak government. An initial conflict between federalists and centralists was succeeded and complicated by the mutual jealousies and suspicions of the Communists and the army, with the result that President Sukarno has spent much of his time and ingenuity in keeping his balance and his office by manoeuvring between these rival forces, while rebellions occur from time to time and a large and potentially prosperous area hovers on the edge of disruption.

The cold war has been a further source of disorders in two different ways. It played a determining part in the insurrections in Azerbaijan and Greece at the end of the second World War, in Malaya from 1948 to 1960, and in the Korean War. In addition it exacerbates other local conflicts and makes them more dangerous and more complicated. The overthrow of the Iraqi monarchy in 1958 and its replacement by a régime partly dependent on Communist support (Brigadier Kassim found himself in a position similar to President Sukarno's in Indonesia) provide an example that needs no elaboration; but even more telling is the case of Cyprus. The core of the Cyprus

problem was the latent conflict between Greeks and Turks, and
this conflict was enlarged to critical proportions by the British
colonial presence and the small military and air bases which the
British maintained on the island. Unlike the root conflict, these
bases were a cold war factor, for by the nineteen fifties Britain
would probably have been prepared to give up Cyprus if there
had been no cold war. So the existence of the cold war caused
the British to adopt an attitude which converted a local dispute
into something much more intractable and extensive, which
was only temporarily [1] resolved when the Greeks and Turks,
scared by the possibility of slaughter, sank their differences behind the backs of the British and then accepted a compromise
whereby the British retained their sovereignty and their bases
in a reduced area.

We come finally to the classic source of interstate quarrels,
disputes over territory or *irredenta*. This cause of war has been in
abeyance in recent years because Europe's irredentist problems
have mostly been solved by force or sweetness (Tirol is the chief
exception), but new conflicts are forming in other parts of the
world as the colonial carpet is taken up to reveal a number of
ill-fitting boards beneath. At present most of the new states with
jagged frontiers are not strong enough to endanger peace by
their territorial dissatisfactions, nor are all these new problems
as menacing as, for instance, Kashmir has been, but this is a
passing phase which may pass quite soon.

The agents of disorder can also be classified in the same rough
and ready way as its sources. The simplest type is the man
moved by personal ambition to try and take a rival's place. His
motives are narrow, but their consequences may not be, for a
coup often turns out to involve more than the fortune of two
individuals and their personal cliques. More often than not the
disorder that starts with a *coup* will contain elements of the deeper
sorts of disorder which we may designate riots and revolutions.

The basic element in a riot is want. It is a manifestation of the
violent indignation of people who are suffering a privation,
usually a material privation, which they feel they ought not to

[1] Temporarily because Greeks and Turks have not been recon-
ciled and the cold war factor has been preserved.

have to suffer. They are implicitly or explicitly accusing their government of incompetence or injustice. Thus the economic policies of the British government during the wars against Napoleon produced such severe hardship in England that the government was eventually faced with a major breakdown of law and order which (having neither a sensible policy nor an adequate police) it could only contain by savage legislation and cavalry charges. One has only to glance round the map of the world today to shudder at the obvious imminence of occurrences of this kind in states which, like the England of Lord Sidmouth and Lord Liverpool, have an inadequate machinery of government set over an inadequately provided body of citizens.

Riots are not revolutions, but they may easily become revolutions. Where a rioter is impelled by want, a revolutionary is impelled by an idea— or he may be a traditionalist reacting against an idea. Riots tend to be comparatively unpremeditated; they are spontaneous or ephemeral responses to a particular situation. But material privations and intellectual ideas do not exist in watertight compartments and it is at least probable that where you have the one, there too you will find the other. In practice a riot is likely to develop into a revolution when the leaders are wittingly or unwittingly appealing to notions as well as emotions, when they have access to arms, and when they are bent on effecting a change of régime. Riots and revolutions have this in common that they occur when the authority has lost the appearance of power and the confidence of a significant section of the community which can no longer wait for redress and believes that something effective can be achieved by a breach of law and order.

II

These are the situations and the men who can disturb the peace and so raise the question whether to intervene or not to intervene. That the larger states can intervene is beyond question. A great power is, almost by definition, a state which has

interests all over the world and the means to promote or protect them. Nor is physical force the only kind of intervention
available. Intervention has many forms and intervention by
force is the wake of disorder is only a last, and often a desperately dangerous, way. Other ways exist and have been sanc-
tioned by the usage of centuries.

We speak now of a British or a French presence or a U.N.
presence as though these things were new, but there is essentially
nothing new about them. States have maintained a presence in
each other's territory ever since the development of communications and of centralized power brought them into permanent
contact with each other, and the object of this presence has been
to obtain information and exert influence. The open agents of
this presence have been diplomats and heads of state, sometimes also extraordinary missions composed of merchants or
monks or debt collectors. Examples abound in the state archives
of Europe and the correspondence of its crowned heads.
Governments have nearly always preferred to get other governments to change their policy or mend their ways by persuasion
rather than by force [1] and the use of argument for this purpose
has never been overlooked or held to be immoral. Modern
methods of communication, especially the radio, provide addi-
tional means of persuasive and continuous intervention.

Economic pressures or inducements are again nothing new.
The novelty lies in the fact that, whereas in the past money used
to be given to key individuals, it is now given to the state as
such (and only passes into the hands of key individuals in part
and unadvisedly). Dollar diplomacy, as it used to be called,
or economic aid, is open to criticism neither on moral nor pragmatic grounds, but because—together with its counterpart of
Russian aid in guns or dams—it has often and unnecessarily
been ill conceived, ill administered and ill fated, and because
it has become part of the armoury of the cold war in that the

[1] This was, of course, easiest where the second government was in
a semi-dependent position. In such a situation (of which an extreme
example is Cromer's Egypt) persuasion could be no more than a
euphemism for force. Unequal treaties and protectorate treaties
enabled the stronger party to keep force out of the argument.

supply of arms or other material imposes creeping obligations on the donees.[1] Economic intervention is a potentially useful tool for keeping the peace. It needs to be refined, not condemned. We shall revert to it.

Armed intervention is itself diverse. Arms have other uses besides employment in battle. They can, for instance, be displayed without being fired. The constant patrols of the American Seventh Fleet in Chinese waters, and the *ad hoc* movements of the same fleet off south-east Asia and of the Sixth Fleet in the eastern Mediterranean are a form of military intervention. French patrols in the western Mediterranean in conjunction with the Algerian war, and the movement of British troops at the time of the Abadan crisis, are likewise inhibitory, even if not everybody would call them peaceable.

Then again weapons of war can be sold rather than used. States make a practice of supplying other states with arms on political calculations (and private individuals indulge in the same trade for non-political reasons). This, too, constitutes a form of intervention. It is regarded as a contribution to stability and peace by donor and donee, and a menace to stability and peace by everybody else, beginning with the neighbours of the donee and the principal opponents of the donor. There are, too, the less conventional forms of military intervention such as the equipment of guerrillas, encouragement of foreign enlistment or connivance at it, and the dispatch of regular forces in the guise of volunteers. And finally there is non-intervention which can be a useful weapon, since a non-intervention agreement may leave a loophole for some kinds of intervention by one side only. If, for example, such an agreement is limited to overt physical intervention, the Russians with their more varied political armoury may turn it to good account by continuing to intervene in other ways peculiar to themselves. Non-intervention agreements tend to be asymmetrical.

The choice is therefore wide. But if a government contemplating intervention concludes that the circumstances warrant

[1] But if it is true (as reported) that spare parts for Migs are now being made in the United States, it will be possible to buy aircraft in the U.S.S.R. and keep them going from other sources.

one kind but not another, it is still not entire master of its policies, for having embarked on one, it may later find itself unable to disengage without becoming embroiled in the other. When the Americans spent $300 million in Laos they hoped that their economic intervention would set the state on its feet and so counter Communist designs and obviate the need for more forceful action, but in the event American aid became one of the ingredients in a developing confusion which led the United States in 1961 to threaten war: where economic intervention had been designed to obviate military intervention, military intervention came to be a corollary of economic intervention.

Finally, we must observe that the form of intervention is affected by the time at which the decision to intervene is taken. Broadly speaking, the sooner the decision the wider the choice. When intervention is postponed, the choice narrows until it becomes one between using armed force and doing nothing. The would-be intervener will then exclaim against the hardness of his lot without drawing attention to the fact that he might have alleviated it, or even avoided the dilemma altogether, by doing something else earlier on. But a major power does not lack the capacity for action. It may lack the resolution; it may, rightly or wrongly, judge that the balance of expediency favours inaction; but the decision whether and how to intervene is not one that need be forced upon it by the circumstances of the moment.

III

What, then, are the factors on either side of the argument? The question that faces a statesman in the context of peace-keeping is whether he should mobilize the resources of his own state and commit them to interference in the affairs of another because some conflict beyond his own borders seems to threaten the peace. Faced with this problem he will need to assess the looming disorder. What does it amount to? Is it perhaps only a little local difficulty? Or is it likely to spread dangerously? There is nothing complicated about the formulation of this question. It is a simple question, but it may be exceedingly difficult to find the answer to it in a particular case, and further-more the statesman has to consider a number of tangential matters which complicate his decision.

The central relevant consideration is this: that intervention is expedient if the disorder, actual or anticipated, is deemed likely to spread and so to cause a major war. Or, put the other way round, do not intervene if the government of the territory involved can deal with the situation.[1] If the dominant object is to keep the peace, then the language riots in India in 1955, for example, did not call for outside intervention, because the government of India never looked like losing control of the situation, but—to go to the other extreme—the collapse of authority in the Congo in 1960 did call for intervention by somebody, because anarchy in the Congo could lead to con-flict between other Africans which could in turn eventually lead to a war between the major powers. Nobody imagined that the Indian language riots could produce a world war. Some people thought the Congo disaster might.

But a state will sometimes intervene for a reason other than keeping the peace, and equally it may hold its hand even though peace might be the better served by intervention. The threat to peace is not the only matter that a national leader has to weigh, for a state has other interests besides peace and it also commonly has obligations. The defence of these interests and the honour-ing of these obligations have in the past led governments to intervene in one way or another in the affairs of other peoples. These are the tangential considerations.

If the intervention contemplated is military, the availability of military force can be decisive. Intervention sometimes has to

---

[1] This applies whether the government is friendly or hostile. If it is friendly and can cope, there is no cause for intervention. If it is hostile and can cope, intervention will be an act of aggression without profit to the insurgents. If intervention would turn the balance against the government, other considerations may arise. But that is no longer a question of keeping the peace.

be immediate to be effective, and if that is so, a state with forces on the spot or within easy range will be strongly tempted to use them even if it is not invited to do so; the British can hardly refrain from intervening if serious disorders break out in Cyprus, so long as they continue to keep troops in the island. On the other hand, a state whose military dispositions are not so apt for intervention will the more easily conclude that it is better to remain passive.

Treaty obligations are another potent factor. It would, for instance, have been difficult for Britain to refuse to go to the aid of King Hussein of Jordan in July 1958, even had there been no ulterior motive,[1] and in 1961 the United States had an awkward time explaining to the Siamese why Seato should not take forceful action in Laos when it could be argued that the circumstances for which the Manila Treaty had been designed had come to pass. A treaty obligation can work two ways. It can give a state which is anxious to intervene an extra and respectable reason for doing so, or it can pull a state into an intervention that it does not wholeheartedly endorse. Either way treaties make for more intervention rather than less, but on the other hand the fashion for multilateral rather than bilateral treaties in the post-war years introduces an element of clumsiness which retards decisions and fosters inaction rather than action.

Treaty obligations are not the same as a fellow feeling for a régime or party in another country, but a fellow feeling often looks like a moral obligation. Thus Britain was thought to owe a debt to the Hashemite line in Iraq and to Nuri-es-Said, and if the revolution of July 1958 had not been over so quickly Britain would have felt some compulsion to intervene on their behalf. Yet it is highly imprudent for one state to have a vested interest in a particular régime in another state and nothing proves this proposition so clearly as the Iraqi case, for Britain came to terms with the revolutionary régime at the first possible opportunity and while it was reputed to be more than half

---

[1] A British failure to respond to the appeal from Jordan would lead the Sheikh of Kuwait and other oil-bearing potentates, with whom Britain had similar treaties, to conclude that Britain was a broken reed.

Communist. Nor was Britain slow to seek relations with the Communist régime in China or so very slow to renew them with President Nasser.

Even in the absence of treaty obligations a state is more likely to intervene in one part of the world than another. This varying sensitivity used to be explained in terms of the doctrine of 'vital interests'. Every state of any consequence at all possesses interests beyond its borders and these interests have customarily been divided into vital interests and non-vital interests. The whole notion is an extremely dubious one. History records few examples of death by loss of vital interests. More usually a state has fought for an interest which it proclaimed to be vital only to discover upon losing it that it was not vital at all. (The British have frequently said that Middle Eastern oil is vital to them, but in 1956 they proved that they could get on without it, at any rate for a time.) Besides economic interests there are strategic interests such as bases, landing rights or over-flying rights, which the beneficiary will be anxious to preserve and which he may even continue to cherish for reasons of prestige after their real usefulness has expired. And finally there are affinities of a vaguer sort. A people which follows the same way of life as another people, which shares its values and has maybe gone through common experiences of the kind that stick in the memory, will not lightly suffer its friends to be assailed without lifting a finger, even though it may have to embark on a hazardous course of action which it would not think of risking on behalf of a more foreign people. There are, of course, strict limits to the operation of such emotions in politics—no European country did anything for the Poles in 1945—but they are not to be entirely discounted, especially in a crisis, as witness the British Dominions' entry into two European great wars and German support for Austria in 1914.

The push and pull of these arguments from interest and obligations has been tautened since the war by certain changes that have come over international affairs. In more distant times the Powers, as they were called, exercised a sort of guardianship of the peace, even though they did so only intermittently and incidentally to their other preoccupations, but the two powers that now tower above their fellows have some reasons for steering clear of the useful officiousness which their predecessors sometimes practised. The first is the well known and well advertised change in the nature of weapons of war. Instead of doing what is required of them modern weapons, we fear, will do a great deal more. We want them in order to deter or, if the worst comes to the worst, to defeat enemies, but we have developed them to the point at which they deter ourselves, so that they have become self-stultifying as political implements and self-destructive as military ones. At the same time we have startlingly increased our command over nature in another direction. We can now travel much faster than ever before and have even begun to travel outside the confines of our own globe and its envelope. Every part of the earth and so every eruption of disorder, wherever it may originate, has acquired political significance: there are no dead areas, nothing in any continent to which we can shut our eyes. The combination of these two achievements of modern science has landed us in a dilemma. On the one hand the business of preventing or containing or resolving disorder has become more urgent, but equally the principal powers have a new reluctance to intervene. The multiplicitly of their concerns, and the appalling consequences of a mistake in appreciation or timing or emphasis, hold them back. Or so it is often assumed.

Ideology increases the haze. In some of the cases I have just cited the notion of semi-sovereignty contributed to an interventionist reaction which can, to this extent, be diagnosed as instinctive, but it is not a complete explanation. A major power may interfere in the affairs of a state within its penumbra out of a mixture of habit (the British case) and quasi-proprietary right (the Russians in Hungary, the Americans in Cuba), but in the last two cases intervention had also ideological springs. In the Russian case these were explicit. Moscow justified its invasion of Hungary on the grounds that the insurrection was bringing a fascist gang to power, thus using an ideological argument in place of appeals to law or national self-defence.[1]

[1] This is not new. The members of the Holy Alliance, for instance, used this sort of language.

Likewise the Americans, when they promoted [1] the invasion of Cuba without any sort of legal pretext, were in effect propounding the view that, in certain parts of the world, Communists can be attacked because they are Communists and even if you have correct relations with them. The United States had recognized the Castro régime, but in the eyes of the administration (or most of it) and of almost the entire American press the United States was right to intervene in Cuba's internal affairs. This was made palatable in public on ideological grounds; the traditional, non-ideological and comprehensible policy of keeping a foreign power out of the Caribbean, which dominated thinking in official circles, was inconspicuous.

We arrive, therefore, at the conclusion that major powers remain particularly liable to fish in disordered waters if the trouble arises in a dependent territory or in a territory which is for one reason or another treated as semi-dependent, and further that the ideological content of the cold war makes for intervention. While dependent territories are dwindling, we cannot say with equal certainty that the tendency to treat sovereign states as less than sovereign is also evaporating, and still less can we predicate an abatement of ideological passion.

We should, in my belief, go further than this and assume that major powers will intervene if any one of three political considerations prevails. First, a major power will intervene if it is, or feels itself to be, directly implicated in an upheaval, the clearest example being Russian involvement in the Hungarian insurrection. Secondly, it will intervene if it is present or can be invoked. Britain is the power which gives most hostages to fortune in this way. Its presence in Cyprus and its treaty with Kuwait are two unsettling illustrations of Britain's persistent inability to untie its own hands. Thirdly, a major power will intervene if it observes a massive build-up by an enemy in an important zone, for it may conclude that, even if it is not directly involved at present, it cannot afford to allow a significant local alteration of power which may come to affect the world balance of power. Here we may cite Laos, where the success of the Pathet Lao all but provoked American armed

[1] Unlike the Russians in Hungary, the Americans sent no troops.

intervention, and we may surmise that if the Americans did not intervene, their abstention was not caused by any complacence about the change in the climate of South East Asia, but by doubts about the willingness of Laotians to fight the Pathet Lao (the Americans did not want to fight alone for obvious propaganda reasons), doubts about Peking's real aims, and ultimately the conviction that the fight would be a losing one.

In sum it is extravagant and contrary to recent experience to assume that the days are over when great powers will intervene in troubles beyond their own borders. Nonetheless, there are powerful reasons for supposing that, outside certain clear emergency cases, they will hesitate to do so and will prefer to encourage intervention of another kind (including if necessary the kind of intervention called non-intervention). There have even been examples of this hesitancy. The British only moved their forces half way to Abadan during the Persian oil crisis and the French preferred not to fight for Tunisia or Morocco; the Russians did not attack Yugoslavia in 1948, either directly or vicariously, nor did they use force in Poland in 1956; General MacArthur was dismissed by President Truman, who refused to take the opportunity to attack China; and the dangers of an enlargement of the Suez and Congo crises were averted. Some of these instances of self-control can be explained in other terms. Britain and France, it may be said, have occasionally recognized the limitations of their post-war status, and the British were inhibited during the Abadan crisis by fear of what might happen to the hundreds of British nationals in the upcountry oilfields of Kuzistan; and the Russian refusal to resort to arms against Yugoslavia was no doubt conditioned by the overconfident expectation that Marshal Tito could easily be overthrown and possibly also by the fact that his refusal to be subordinated to Moscow occurred while the Americans still had a monopoly of nuclear weapons. But alongside these particular factors certain general considerations have been present.

We have already considered the fear of nuclear weapons. This is an undoubted restraint. There is, further, the fact that the genuinely military interests of the European powers (other than the U.S.S.R.) round the world have declined, while the

United States has found in mobile fleets and abundant funds alternative and more subtle ways of securing their strategic and political interests without having to acquire territorial bases. Although far-away events attract universal attention and have long-range repercussions,[1] the possession of distant territory has become less valuable, and the leaders of the more powerful states conduct their external relations with more regard to the goodwill of foreign governments and peoples and less preoccupation about foreign bases. At the same time the principal powers have found themselves compelled to compete for the favour of third parties, as the weight of the uncommitted has grown in international politics and the domination of the giants has been neutralized by their mutual frustration. And it is not possible to get this favour by interfering in other people's affairs. Force in international politics has become to some extent self-defeating. Force impresses—but not always favourably. A show of force, it used to be said, was something the lesser breeds could understand. But they never liked it. And now that they see two shows of force in stalemate, they fear force less and are the freer to react against it. The use of force by the Russians in Hungary seriously damaged the Russians in, for example, India, and both giants are now compelled to exercise restraint so long as they attach importance to the competition between them for the suffrages of others.

But above all there are certain severely practical limitations on the use of force in modern conditions. It is almost true to say that timing is all. The proposed American intervention at Dien Bien Phu and the Anglo-French attack on Egypt are both examples of action that was fatally delayed. The British landing at Kuwait, on the other hand, was long anticipated and briskly executed; there was no opposition and therefore no prior need to seize airfields and harbours. But had the British been compelled to undertake preparatory operations of this kind, or had they not been invited in by the Sheikh in good time, it is doubtful whether they would have acted at all. Mr. Macmillan stated that the decision to land forces in Kuwait was only reached with

[1] This circumstance is not new. The Seven Years War started in America, a remote spot.

difficulty and we may therefore suppose that any extra complication could easily have tipped the scales the other way. In the event the British expedition had the twin advantages of previous planning and freedom from opposition. This combination of circumstances is rare.[1]

The absence of opposition is unpredictable, but some preparatory planning is possible. In areas covered by multilateral or bilateral treaties discussions are continuous and exercises frequent; they are indeed one of the prime purposes of Nato, Cento and Seato. But other areas, notably India, Burma, and Africa as a whole, are untouched by defence treaties and less well covered by contingency planning, and the likelihood of intervention is thereby reduced. In the Congo the U.N.'s intervention was not in the first place conceived as a military operation, and the lack of planning was offset by the absence of any determined opposition.

Timing is also affected by the nature of the disorder which it is sought to stifle or contain. If the threat is an internal and not an external one, it is exceedingly difficult to ensure timely intervention. A government in trouble will not invite outside aid, since to do so is an admission of failure; it will wait until its fortunes are so low that it has ceased to worry about its prestige, and that is a very low point and a desperately late one. In any case intervention against an internal threat is specially difficult, since the need is for policemen who understand the local language, and outsiders—unable to provide such a force—are therefore dissuaded from intervening.

The possession of overseas bases and garrisons is both an element in timing and a great deal more. For historical reasons Britain has had, and still to some extent retains, bases from which it can despatch men and material to diverse parts of the world, whereas the United States with a different history has recourse to allied as opposed to colonial bases and can afford the expensive alternative of afloat support. Besides enabling a government to launch an operation a base contains the hospitals

[1] So is the practicability of getting out again almost at once. Unlike the unhappy Gladstone after Tel el Kebir, Mr. Macmillan was able to extricate himself.

and repair shops which may be required as it proceeds—and the nearer the better. Sea transport over long distances is slow; air transport is inadequate for heavy equipment and encounters the legal barrier of national sovereignties if the air route lies over the territory of states which do not want to become involved or which sympathize with the country under attack.

Nor is the value of a base confined to the ready access which it guarantees to trouble spots, or even to the provision of hospital accommodation and repair shops close to the scene of action. It is also a place where men can be acclimatized and matured. It is not possible to send men straight from Salisbury Plain to action in the Persian Gulf without the certainty that a high proportion of them will soon be in hospital; the satisfactory medical record of the Kuwait excursion in 1961 was due to the fact that nearly all the troops went from Cyprus, Aden, and Nairobi, and very few from the United Kingdom. When the British policed the world or a good part of it, they possessed two nuclei of power, the British army at home and the British army in India plus the Indian army. India, and the outlying bases acquired as a result of British dominion in India, provided acclimatization. The abandonment of India constituted one of the most drastic changes in a strategic picture that has ever been effected at a stroke, and the consequent, if gradual, loss of other bases is emphasizing the inability of Britain to intervene by force all over the world. The opportunities lost to Britain are also opportunities lost to its friends and allies.[1]

The successor states of the British Empire and of every other colonial system are anxious above all to delete the more obtrusive symbols of their past subservience. A military garrison or base is therefore one of the first things to liquidate, even though there may be sensible arguments for its retention. It seems, for instance, inconceivable at the time of writing this book that the Kenya base can survive the declaration of Kenyan independence notwithstanding that it brings £3 million a year to the

---

[1] But perhaps the friends and allies might to some extent remedy the loss. There are jungles and deserts in Australia, Malaya, North Borneo, Bechuanaland, and the United States.

country, that its disappearance may accelerate the flight of
white settlers, and that its retention would help to keep independent Kenya's own defence expenditure down. Nigeria, too,
has reasons for having a British establishment, but the reasons
against doing so are stronger and will surely prevail. In
Malaya, it is true, the Malayan defence agreement permits the
retention of British garrisons (but British military facilities may
not be used for the direct support of Seato) and Pakistan has
accepted military commitments. But these examples should not
mislead. No independent state will accept a base which, like
Aden, may be used for any purpose chosen by the occupier. If
Pakistan accepts British support, it will do so only for the defence of Pakistani interests by reason of Pakistani fears (of India,
for example) and not for any purely British or American purpose. Moreover, the state which looks to another state for help
prefers its ally's forces to be near at hand rather than on its very
soil, so that state A wishes to be succoured from state B, B from
C and so on. If this pattern of emotions holds true, if Kuwait
hopes for help in an emergency from Aden but refuses to have
even a single British battalion on its own soil beforehand, then
there will be no places for foreign bases except remote, expensive and inadequate islands like Gan and St. Helena, and the
likelihood of intervention is once again on practical grounds
diminished.

IV

We have proceeded so far on the basis that disorder is in-
variably a bad thing and that Western governments are in-
variably weakened by its occurrence and should devote full
attention and ingenuity to preventing or containing it. Both
assumptions need to be examined.

In the first place it is important not to confuse disorder with
change, although the two frequently go together. It is evident
that change is sometimes good in itself and/or favourable to the
West. Thus the overthrow of Perez Jimenez in Venezuela in
January 1958 was, *pace* certain pessimistic businessmen, a

change to be welcomed rather than deplored; the Western reaction to the fall of King Farouk was favourable; the dislodge-
ment of either of the Iberian dictators could not *per se* be said
to be a disadvantage for the West; and the fall of Dr. Verwoerd
would undoubtedly be regarded by countless Westerners as a
contribution to the good of mankind. In the nineteenth century
the British in particular abetted change, including violent
change, in many parts of Europe, and they supported revolution not only to embarrass their adversaries among the Powers
but also on liberal and humanitarian grounds. The Americans
have been no less radical, as witness their support for Latin
American insurgents against Spain and for Irish and Indian
insurgents against Britain. This spirit is not extinct, but the
West has become increasingly preoccupied with the need to
control change and prevent it from harming a system, a code
and a civilization which were taken for granted in the nineteenth century, but can be so no longer.

Change may be welcome, but it is also dangerous. For Britain
it is more dangerous than it used to be because Britain is in a
comparatively less dominant position in the world and has
therefore lost some of its power to control the course of events.
For the West as a whole it is dangerous because the dice of
change look as though they are loaded against the West. The
place of Western liberalism as a social catalyst has been partially usurped by Communism, with the result that change seems
likely, and disorder very likely, to redound to Communist advantage. Change and disorder are therefore abjured by the
West, which equates internal upheavals with Communist opportunity [1] and is pathologically quick to label any new figure
on the world stage a Communist or nearly so; too many of the
new rulers in Asia and Africa have been misinterpreted in this
way. And the rise of Communism as the pseudo-liberator of the

[1] The fear that France and Italy might go Communist played a
part in the birth of Nato. But the main object was to revive Western
Europe and recreate a counterpoise to the Russians. In this context the Prague *coup* was more important than Communist strikes
in France and Italy. The Prague *coup* also transformed Western
policy in Germany from the dismantling to the rebuilding phase.

underprivileged has pushed the West into alliance with régimes, often incompetent and reactionary as well as unpopular, whom in the last resort Western popular opinion is not too keen to salvage and Western governments believe in their hearts to be half-way to the rubbish dump.

There is, moreover, a fundamental sense in which the West is at a disadvantage. While there are some things that should inhibit both sides equally—international opinion against intervention, especially armed intervention, has become harder and more articulate—there are other considerations which specially affect the West. Russian intervention is relatively cheap, unobtrusive and domestically painless. The constant parades of American fleets in distant waters are extremely expensive and have to be paid for by the American taxpayer, while at the same time they are comparatively inefficient in terms of the threats which they may have to meet. The Russians do not use their own troops except in the U.S.S.R.'s immediate penumbra; Hungary apart, no Russian soldier has been killed abroad since 1945. The Russians, who stand to gain from disorders for precisely the reasons for which the West fears them, can exploit them invisibly, whereas the suppression or containing of disorder entails the dispatch of troops to the accompaniment of the rumble of headlines. The consequences of this balance of disadvantages to the West can be seen in the fact that the area in which Communists hesitate to intervene has shrunk.

For most practical purposes intervention means intervention in the uncommitted parts of the world. Disturbances within the spheres of Communist dominance illumine the discontent of the inhabitants and bring the West some benefit (e.g. hostile Asian reactions against Russian intervention in Hungary and the Chinese invasion of Tibet), but they do not lead to Western intervention. Similarly Communist disorders in, say, France or Italy would be gratifying to the Russians, but would not produce direct Russian intervention. Some propaganda and perhaps a little financial help are all that the trouble-makers on either side can expect. But in the uncommitted areas the situation is more open. Even when, as in the Congo, there is little positive advantage in intervening, there is a strong temptation

to do so, and it is easy for a power which takes the first step to
become more heavily involved than it intended and unable to
extricate itself without loss of face or even loss of political stakes.
Yet in this dangerous area Western intervention is even more
quickly resented and more easily misinterpreted than Russian
or Chinese intervention, for the simple and well known reason
that the West once ruled these roosts. The West starts with a
handicap.

It is, moreover, difficult for the West to intervene. Western
governments operate in open societies which are used to asking
questions, taking different sides and keeping a close watch on
how the government spends its money. A democratic government may be held back by a divided public opinion or the prospect of dividing it, while even in the case of clandestine intervention a democratic government has to bear in mind that
secrets are not always kept and that money spent has to be accounted for. In Communist countries there may be disagree-
ments within the governing hierarchy, but there are no popular
outcries against policy nor any inquiry into motives or manage-
ment. The people is hardly, if at all, a factor. In a democracy,
however, the people is a factor and frequently a restraining
one. Consequently the case for intervention has to be strong
and simple and comprehensible.

There is no popular opposition to diplomatic intervention
(as opposed to criticism, usually ill informed, of diplomats), but
there is some opposition to spending money for foreign political
purposes and massive opposition to a recourse to arms. People
who are prepared to give for specific purposes, such as relief
for refugees or the victims of a particular flood or famine or for
the South African treason trial, are much less willing to give
their government a blanket authority to spend large sums annu-
ally on less obviously urgent causes and less obviously personal
purposes. The usefulness of economic intervention in the affairs
of other people—usefulness, that is, to the givers as well as the
recipients—has been less well publicized or understood than
the many mistakes and instances of peculation and ingratitude
that have marked the history of this kind of international activity. Moreover, fatal flaw, the objects of economic aid have been

confused. Is it intended to secure clients or peace? We shall return to this topic in the next chapter.

The use of force is even more unpalatable to popular opinion than the use of gold and favours. The manifest risks of nuclear war are no doubt apparent on both sides of the iron curtain, but they are in the nature of things more effective politically in countries where the people as well as the rulers claim a voice in the making of policy and the spending of public funds. While it is true that in the United States there is virtually no opposition to defence expenditure—Congress has more than once forced money on the Administration for a particular weapon—the less affluent and less ideologically conscious countries of Western Europe are apt to be more gruding with their money and also less ready to sanction political risks.

It follows that the Western statesman is in a special dilemma when faced with disorder. He may conclude that it is expedient to intervene with force, but he has to ask himself whether his intervention may not be unpopular at home. If he is robust or confident (and in command of a sound parliamentary majority) he will go ahead, but if he is weak in character or control he may falter. He may, of course, conclude that popular opinion in a democracy is not inevitably pacific. It has its belligerent phases. A substantial segment—some say a majority—of British opinion approved Sir Anthony Eden's assault on Egypt in 1956, and American opinion was at least as favourable to the invasion of Cuba in 1961. But a democratic leader (in his right mind) will at least have to pause and give more thought to the state of opinion at home than a Communist leader needs to do.

One alternative to the use of national force is international intervention under the aegis of the United Nations (to which we will return), but Western leaders in Europe have failed to generate much confidence in the United Nations among their publics and will themselves be unwilling to resort to it unless the issues involved are peripheral to their own country's main interests. Initially the French in Algeria and the British in Cyprus and the Dutch in Indonesia stubbornly opposed the 'internationalization' of their troubles in these areas. They may become more internationally minded when their own prerogatives are not so directly challenged, but for the time being they represent a class which, having lost power, is unwilling to entrust it to anybody else. Thus these middling powers are inhibited, and the giant powers in some areas are mutually restrained, at the moment when the international scene is suddenly peopled with a hustle of new-comers.

Chapter 3

The Instability of New States

NEW states tend to be weak but not meek. New states are not necessarily small states, as witness India, Nigeria, the Congo; nor are they necessarily without resources, witness Malaya, Kuwait. But emerging as they do from foreign tutelage they lack certain things and are in consequence less stable than they would otherwise be.

The instability of a state may become a threat to peace either by causing a civil war in that state, or by turning the minds of its rulers to aggressive designs in order to bolster up their régime, or by tempting a predatory neighbour, or by creating an anarchic condition which will prompt the intervention of the protagonists in the cold war. New states are not the only, or always the most, unstable states, nor is a state necessarily more dangerous when it is unstable than when it is stable—stability may be a prerequisite and an encouragement to expansiveness—but it so happens that at the present time instability is a more obvious source of trouble than stability and that much of this instability arises in new states and is well exemplified by their problems.

The deficiencies of new states exist on two planes. First, they lack apparatus and symbols. They are short of administrators and professional men and women as well as national anthems, national armies, and national banks. Their wants vary in urgency, but in every case they require, and know they require, skills and materials and institutions, which their former governors have provided sparsely or not at all. Secondly, they lack assurance. They are not only conscious of the inadequacy of their equipment, but also doubtful of the respect of the international society into which they have graduated and overanxious to play their part and prove their worth. New states are not to be accounted *ipso facto* a greater threat to peace than their older brethren, nor would I wish to give any encouragement to the curious view that big wars have in the past been caused by small states, but the new states' tendency to instability presents a special problem. Their number is alarming. Since the war Asia and Africa have contributed fifteen and twenty-five new members respectively to the family of independent nations, and the next ten years could produce yet more at an average rate of one a year. This increase makes the area of potential instability alarmingly great, all the more so since many of these states have little or none of the cohesiveness of older states, but are unnatural products of alien rule and historical accident. They are not states of the same kind as the nation states of Europe, which have either matured slowly over centuries (Britain, France, Spain, Portugal, Denmark, Sweden) or have had their forms pre-conditioned by their neighbours (Italy, Germany); the bonds of the new states are made for bursting. An international society containing some three dozen members whose entity is more formal than real is a very different society from any that the world has ever known. All the states of the world are now in permanent contact with each other, and I do not think that there has ever been a time when one-third of the members of a continuously consorting group have been in a state of upheaval within uncertain frontiers. For it is not only the boundaries of these new states that are fluid. Their society in itself is inchoate. To emerge from tutelage is a sufficiently traumatic experience, but to emerge from technological innocence into the twentieth century is a shock so violent that it can hardly be appreciated by anybody who has not suffered it. Old customs, habits, beliefs, values, and rules become irrelevant; an *élite* gropes for new ones, while the mass is left with none. A great gulf opens between the *élite* and the rest, greater perhaps—because more unacceptable—than the old gap between colonial masters and subject races. And pervading the whole scene are poverty and inexperience, sometimes on a staggering scale.

The poverty and the inexperience can be relieved, and this relief will make it easier for distraught societies to find a new equilibrium. But we have not yet painted the whole picture. The problem is more than a problem of giving material comfort to societies in the throes of transformation. There is also a wider context. These societies struggling with an intimidating present and a baffling future find themselves acting in a world of international politics where they have important interests, inherited prejudices, and some influence. Moreover, this interaction between newer states and older, between the poorer and the richer, is complicated by the coincidence that the older and the richer are themselves ranged in two hostile arrays. There is therefore no joint programme for giving aid according to need, and there is competition for cold war advantages in Asia and Africa.

The dominant prejudice of new states in their dealings with the rest of the world is their inbred antipathy to the old colonial powers. It is difficult to assess the force of this prejudice. Businessmen from former colonial powers often find a genuinely ready welcome and the British Royal family a genuinely enthusiastic one; visits of both kinds reveal and strengthen the good that has come of the old relationship. But the roots of distrust are there, too, and both sides find it fatally easy to judge each other by the worst of what they see rather than the best. Thus, to the African one Western European is much like another; they are all white colonialists with minor variations, just as a thousand years ago they were all Franks to Alexius Comnenus. In fact, the colonial powers, whose empires in Asia and Africa are now extinct or doomed, had quite different preconceptions about colonies, although in the end they all made much the same mistake about timing. The Belgians behaved as though they thought—and in this they seem to have followed Marx, albeit unwittingly—that so long as they gave economic benefits, everybody would be happy and the enjoyment of colonies would continue indefinitely. The Dutch did not awake to the possibility of being parted from their possessions until the middle of the second World War and the Portuguese have successfully resisted thinking about it at all. The British, wittingly or unwittingly following Turgot's maxim that colonies were like fruit which ripens and then falls off the branch, usually regarded colonies as temporary possessions, and accepted a degree of responsibility for their care and maintenance during the fructifying period,[1] but even they thought that they had much more time than proved to be the case, and were slow to realize that what was done in India in 1947 was to be repeated in Africa in the same generation and not in the next. The French gave a great deal of thought, during and after the second World War, to the future of the French empire, but, although they won a breathing-space and used it to extend and intensify their influence by an adroit exploitation of air communications and very considerable investment, they ruined the effect in the short term by their behaviour in Guinea and Algeria. Nevertheless it is French rule which may turn out in the long run to have been the most fruitful, since the French interpreted colonial responsibility as something that went beyond the tutelage and training which the British felt bound to provide. Although faced with essentially the same problems as the British and other colonial rulers, French policy had an extra dimension, and aimed from the beginning to make a cultural impact as well as to perform the more obvious tasks of government and facilitate the broader paths of commerce. For this reason there may be a community of understanding a generation hence between France and its former dependencies which will be missing in the other states born in the mid-twentieth century. In our own day, however the chief feature of all colonial partings has been haste, and consequently the preparation of colonies for independence has, with the striking exception of Malaya, everywhere borne the stamp not so much of experienced and wise European governors (though there were some such), but of strenuously militant nationalist movements, staking their pride upon a timetable and forming new states in the image of a revolutionary movement.

A second important factor is the impact of the cold war in this generation of colonial emancipation. Practically every new state has opted for neutrality and as the number of new states has grown, so has the number of neutrals. Moreover, this increase in the ranks of the uncommitted coincided with an

[1] This was the dominant British attitude in the first half of the nineteenth century and much of the twentieth. It is perhaps not true of the imperialism of the latter part of the nineteenth century.

increase in their importance for quite a different reason. With the ending of the American nuclear monopoly the cold war was transformed to the considerable advantage of the non-combatants, for the equivocal strategic balance of the major powers forced them to pay greater attention to lobbying neutrals. Neutrality even became a positive policy in place of a negative withdrawal, as the neutrals' consciousness of their new weight in international affairs encouraged them to try to influence the course of great events. In spite of differences on many matters Asian and African states co-operated at the United Nations and consciously sought to increase their unity and their prominence in the series of conferences which began with the Afro-Asian conference at Bandung in 1955 and has extended so far to the conference of twenty-four neutrals held at Belgrade in September 1961. Half of these twenty-four states had come into existence since 1945. Their juniority and their attitude towards the cold war were about their only common characteristics. They were a collection of new states alarmed by the prospect of a world war started by older and greater states. Their influence was marginal and indirect; on specific major issues like Berlin and disarmament it was very limited indeed, but in a general way the neutrals could feel that in their own continents their wishes had to be reckoned with. Their material needs and their psychological discomforts were to some extent balanced by political assets.

There is a sizeable literature on the subject of economic and technical aid to underdeveloped countries. We cannot here enter in any detail into that field, but equally we cannot ignore it, for there is no subject more important for keeping the peace than the prevention of the disorders which are bred by want. In the next chapter we shall have much to say about the United Nations, but everything that has to be said under that heading will refer to the containment or repression of disorder, not to prevention. Apart from the cold war, the greatest danger to peace is probably the instability of poor states (most of which are also new states) and there is no doubt that, given a proper understanding and the political will, many of the sources of their instability could be eliminated. It is therefore necessary for a study like this to survey problems of economic aid in a general way before dealing more particularly with the kinds of aid which are specially pertinent to our theme, namely military and police aid.

II

A state makes an uncomfortable neighbour when distracted or depressed by poverty or driven asunder by centrifuge. It is therefore to the general advantage that states should be reasonably prosperous and coherent, that the inhabitants should have a sense of satisfaction and a sense of belonging. But in most countries the people have little enough cause for either and the world is lucky if societies are resigned and indifferent where they could so easily be in ferment and fragmentation. Modern politics are based on the idea of society as nation, and a nation has been defined as a 'materially and morally integrated society, with a stable and enduring authority at the centre, with fixed frontiers, and with a relative moral and spiritual and cultured unity shared by those who consciously belong to the state and accept its laws': [1] integration, not agglomeration. Disintegrated nations are a source of instability in international society. This is the pragmatic justification for foreign aid which is a distribution of goods, services and capital in return for an expectation of greater tranquillity. Before independence a colonial overlord can do various things on the political plane, as the British did in Malaya, to create an integrated society and a sense of nationhood. After independence politics become the affair of the peoples of the emancipated state, but outsiders may still exert influence, diplomatic and above all economic, with the object of consolidating the new state.

All states are developing and most of them are by common consent underdeveloped. The rich minority is developing much faster than the rest, with the result that the gap between the

[1] M. Mauss in *La Nation*. 'L'Année sociologique (1953–54)', Paris, 1957, p. 17

most and the least favoured is increasing all the time. At present all that foreign aid does is to prevent an even greater acceleration of the discrepancy. Among the rich there is a conflict between the urge to go on getting richer and the feeling, part guilt and part political calculation, that some of the increase in wealth ought to be spread abroad. Among the poor is a sense of urgency which comes partly from below where there is a new awareness that poverty is not an inescapable lot, and partly from above when politicians discover that they must either produce goods or be turned out.

The giving of aid raises three main questions: To whom? What kind of aid? Where from?

Aid may be given first to the poorest. Or it may be given to countries under greatest Communist or other obnoxious pressure. Or to those best able to use it. Or to those whose stability will have an effect beyond their own borders. In practice some aid will be given in all these categories. The very poor, like Somalia, cannot be gainsaid, but what they receive is not much; their own compass is small. The political criterion will certainly have some weight. The economic judgement has had even greater weight, as the volume of aid given to India shows. Perhaps the last argument has been the least influential, and if this has indeed been the case it deserves greater attention. In Africa the fortunes of Nigeria, the Sudan and Kenya will have a decisive bearing on the future of all Africa, and the case for helping them as much as possible is an uncommonly strong one. There is, too, a question whether to concentrate aid in a few places, for whatever reason those places may be selected, or to distribute it more widely in order to please as many people as possible.

The choice between the forms of aid is equally un-clear cut. The greatest initial impact is made by large projects such as the Russians have favoured—the high dam at Aswan, a hospital in Cambodia, a stadium in Indonesia. But for the West to compete in kind would be shortsighted. Western helpers should concentrate on getting as many first-class individuals as possible to the needy countries and should lay the emphasis on technical as opposed to capital aid (even though some recipients may regard technical aid as a way of evading substantial capital disbursements) : to provide and train doctors and nurses; find university and secondary-school teachers; give technical, vocational and administrative training on the spot or in Western institutions; support institutes and stations for training in agricultural, medical and veterinary services, and other skills which people intending to work in tropical countries must learn in tropical countries; advise on the institution and functioning of a proper judical system; help to finance and direct research —in a word convert colonial services into services suited to independent countries and expand them. There are two distinct ways of getting men for such tasks—secondment for relatively short stretches, and a service with longer and less definite horizons. Secondment is the more suitable method for recruiting the technicians which are needed in the more advanced countries like India, where the kind of expert needed changes year by year. In education, too, a regular secondment system would provide openings for men and women who want to see something of the world before settling down (the pre-war short-service scheme of the R.A.F. did something of the kind), provided that five years' overseas service comes to mean a good mark and not a loss of opportunity and promotion. There is also a case for a corps of permanent or semi-permanent servants who are willing to spend longer periods away from home as members of a service like the old colonial services. The difficulties have often been rehearsed: a colonial service provided a career with honour, security and pension, and the cost of the service was borne by the local and not by the metropolitan taxpayer. No substitute has yet been found (although the tentative Commonwealth Technical and Advisory Service may be a beginning in the states emerging from British rule), but it is over-pessimistic to assume that the spirit of adventure and service has suddenly disappeared and that an efficiently organized and aptly inspired service would fail to find recruits.

The two great all-comprehending needs of emergent territories are in health and education. If the medical services collapse and plagues develop, there could be an exodus which would halt development and throw a country back into the jungle. In education it was the custom of colonial régimes to regard schooling as a luxury which might be given to some people some day when the territory could afford it, but today this doctrine has been completely reversed and it is now universally preached that there can be no advances without education. Priorities are a source of debate, but it is probably true to say that those who are knowledgeable in these matters put secondary education before primary on the grounds that, while the latter is not too glaringly inadequate, the former is signally failing to produce enough children qualified to proceed to universities and colleges to be trained for the public service and the professions, including the teaching profession itself. Although these skills may to some extent be imported, there are limits at both ends, since the more advanced countries have no large exportable surplus and the needy countries will not tolerate more than a certain proportion of foreigners in key positions.

Whence are these needs to be met? After the war some colonial powers woke up to their responsibilities. The British, and still more the French, increased their expenditure in a well intentioned, if tardy, attempt to repair the omissions of the past, but their colonial time was short. Aid from Western Europe continues, although on terms that have hardly yet been rationalized,[1] and far greater sums are now being spent by the United States and the U.S.S.R., largely within the terms of the cold war. The outstanding contribution has, of course, been the American. The great post-war programme of American military and economic aid has been a pioneer venture in the use by a national government of a special kind of strength, namely economic strength, in order to promote national ends,

---

[1] When Ghana became independent it was discovered that fresh British legislation was needed in order to sanction the continuance of works in progress under colonial development schemes. Some £350,000 was thereafter spent in Ghana in this way, chiefly on the Kumasi College of Technology. The University of Dakar continues to be financed by the French and other universities in the former French possessions are projected; each territory has an École Nationale d'Administration for the training of officials. Several thousand Frenchmen are still working in former French African colonies and in Morocco and Tunisia.

of which keeping the peace may be one. Like all pioneering ventures it has had its achievements and its shortcomings. The conduct of national policy by the deployment of cash and goods has been at times confused, because there is an underlying duality of purpose. In the late forties and early fifties American aid was primarily designed to put Europe on its feet. When aid was extended to Asia and the Middle East this simple objectivity was complicated for a few years by the doctrine that aid was a way of securing and rewarding allies, but before the end of President Eisenhower's term of office the original purpose of strengthening independent states had been reasserted. President Kennedy has made this reversion to first principles more explicit. But the confusion and suspicion sown in the mid-fifties have not all been blown away and Washington is still accused of mixing its motives. Is aid intended to win neutral states to the American side or to alleviate poverty in order to eliminate possible sources of unrest? In the former case the aim is strength, in the latter peace. The two aims may coincide, but equally they may not. Nor will onlookers necessarily diagnose the aims correctly or charitably, so that a grantor, however benevolent, is always suspected of giving aid at least as much for his own benefit as for the good of the recipient.

Besides competing for the suffrages of the undetermined, the dispensers of aid wish to bolster the military usefulness of their friends, whether by supplying arms, or by building such things as roads and factories which have their uses in peace as well as war, or by raising a local standard of living with a view to reducing the risk of the overthrow of an allied régime by popular revolution; and all these things act as a deterrent to enemies to the extent to which they win and strengthen friends. The American programme began when the British government decided in 1946 that it could no longer go on supporting Greece and Turkey economically. The United States stepped in with special measures to help these two countries (1947–9) and soon expanded its economic foreign policy with the Marshall Plan (1948–50) and its successors, the Mutual Defence Assistance Programme (1949–51) and the Mutual Security Programme (1952 onwards). The M.S.P. aims to nourish the economies of less developed parts of the free world (upon which the United States is becoming increasingly dependent, as the Paley and Draper reports have emphasized); to give economic help to military allies who, being 'under the gun', have to maintain larger military establishments than they can themselves afford; and to give special assistance in particular political or economic causes such as the support of Berlin or Jordan, the control of malaria or the succour of refugees. The programme has been much criticized, especially within the United States, but most of the criticism has been directed against the way the programme has been elaborated and administered rather than against the basic idea of spending large sums of money in foreign aid as an adjunct of American foreign policy.

Various claims are made on behalf of that policy. First there is a group of direct cold war propositions: that foreign aid is an essential ingredient in a foreign policy based on a global deterrent; that it has helped to counter Russian subversion and intimidation; that the $20 billion contributed to allied forces in the fifties was better spent that way than on American military establishments; that American aid ensured Western Europe's recovery, laid the basis for its self-defence and prevented France, Italy, and Berlin from falling to the Communists. Further, it is argued that the policy has kept the peace. Countries like Greece and Turkey, Iran and the Philippines have had stability (or more stability than they would have had), and the whole Nato area has remained at peace; in the areas covered by Seato and Cento it has been possible to keep nuclear weapons in reserve because local economies and military forces have been strengthened. Finally, there is the claim that the provision of foreign aid, especially defence support funds for power and hygiene and communications, has significantly influenced inherently revolutionary areas and caused them to move, since move they must, in the direction of ordered development instead of towards violence and anarchy.

All these arguments can be conceded without meeting the major criticisms which have been advanced against American aid. There have been instances of conspicuous expenditure followed by decided reverses. Laos provides the obvious ex-

ample. Here the Americans spent $300 million in order to keep
the country from going the same way as North Vietnam, and
yet within five years of the Geneva conference of 1954 the pro-
Communist Pathet Lao was probably the strongest single force
in the country and the pro-Western government was incapable
of maintaining itself. There were also other cases where the
political return on the sums expended seemed disappointingly
small, if not completely elusive.

The commonest explanation of this sort of fiasco was to ac-
cuse the United States of political ineptitude and unimagina-
tiveness—or in other words, to say that it had intervened in the
right place at the right time, but in the wrong way. In some
cases it could be accused of giving the wrong kind of aid, e.g.
obsolescent American weapons that were too complicated for
the recipients or unsuited to local conditions (but sometimes
the fault lay with the recipients themselves, who specified the
weapons they wanted with more of an eye to their appearance
than their usefulness). Then again, the purpose of the aid was
not always properly thought out. Some postulants wanted it in
order to build up a gendarmerie; others because they had a
local enemy, e.g. Pakistan, in which case the provision of aid
could do more to increase than to cure local tension; some
wanted to stand up to the Russians; others to strengthen their
own military class, with consequences which might be bene-
ficial to peace or to freedom or to both or to neither.

On the American side there was confusion between building
up allies and fostering neutralism. John Foster Dulles abhorred
neutrals, but even before his death in 1959 it was becoming
apparent in Washington that some countries could not be
turned into effective allies and that their neutrality was in
any case all that could reasonably be desired. The American
failure in Laos, where Washington backed a régime which was
not in the last resort prepared to fight, has become a classic
instance of political bad judgement. The Americans mistook
the nature of their clients and failed to see that the Laotian
princes and generals of their choice knew little and cared less
about the outside world, and in these circumstances it was
foolish to imagine that the American camp or the cause of

freedom would be strengthened by disbursing funds in a country without any public opinion in favour of either Americans or freedom. More blantantly, dictatorial Latin American recipients of United States hardware abused it, so that Washington's intentions in giving it were inevitably held up to public censure in freer parts of the world; some inherently unstable local dispensation was given an extra but still limited lease of life, but no long term United States interest was served and in the wider world the American image was damaged.

If the United States has oscillated between two fixed ideas, the Russians have used economic aid where they saw a chance for political gain and largely by way of riposte to American aid, giving aid to the neighbours of countries receiving American aid (e.g. to Egypt and Syria after the conclusion of the Baghdad Pact and to Afghanistan in the same context). These countries, with Indonesia, have received more aid from the U.S.S.R. than from the West and (with the possible exception of Outer Mongolia) lead the list of countries that have received Russian aid. In the competition for the goodwill of third parties, and for influence in uncommitted states, economic aid has become an increasingly important weapon; especially in poor countries, money talks. Through trade and aid the Russians have tried to supplant Western powers and to step in when they make mistakes. In this context aid to nationalist leaders is more fruitful than sending arms and advice to Communist bands and cells.

The use of economic strength in international affairs, and economic intervention in the affairs of other countries, have only secondary (if any) peace-keeping effects where the aid is given by major powers whose primary concern is their own antagonism. American aid did bring health and wealth and strength to Western Europe, but it was not this kind of American intervention which kept the Russians from falling upon Western Europe, nor was it any kind of American aid which kept the Western Europeans at peace among themselves. In the Middle East aid—whether Anglo-Saxon under the Baghdad Pact or French to Israel or Russian to Egypt—may incidentally have contributed to a precarious peace by piling up a balance of armaments at a forbidding level, but the mainspring of these programmes has not been the desire of the donors to foster the prosperity and coherence which are essential requisites for the stability of a state and therefore for the stability of a world order based on states.

Aid given for the wrong reasons or in the wrong way may be better than no aid, and it is useless to expect that the antagonists in the cold war are going to give aid without any reference to their fearful mutual preoccupations. Nevertheless the cold war taint of their foreign aid is a flaw. To some Americans and all Russians the idea that foreign aid should be divorced from the cold war sounds absurd. Yet to the great majority of those who live in underdeveloped countries this same idea is an axiom.

The obvious way to take the cold war out of aid is to channel aid through the United Nations or other international or un-committed bodies. Aid given in this way (besides helping in-cidentally to make new states feel that they have a real stake in the U.N.) will increase and is specially apposite for certain purposes. There is, for example, a strong case for a U.N. capital development fund to help new states to acquire a sound infrastructure of hospitals, transport, etc., and the F.A.O.'s food surplus scheme is one way of at least holding living stan-dards at their present level in the face of the menace of increas-ing populations (though economic aid on the present scale is unlikely to be able to do more than that). But aid through the U.N. is subject to grave impediments and is unlikely to be any-thing like as plentiful as bilateral aid for many years to come. U.N. agencies are by no means completely shielded from cold-war currents, the very size of the U.N. is an obstacle to effi-ciency, and the practice of requiring U.N. posts to be allocated on a geographical basis means that good men must sometimes be passed over in favour of less good. But an even more pertinent limitations on the use of U.N. channels for aid is the fact that these channels are still very narrow. Although the total amount of aid provided by all U.N. agencies exceeds the aid given by any single country except the United States, this total is dis-persed over a great variety of projects and purposes. The Tech-nical Assistance Board provides advice and foreign aid, and OPEX deploys executives, but these schemes only touch the fringe of the problem; the latter's recruits number fewer than 100. The Special Fund, at present directed by Mr. Paul Hoffmann, conducts pre-investment surveys, and the new International Development Association has been brought into existence to promote schemes which the International Bank, obliged by its rules to lend only on commercial terms, must eschew. And there are the Specialized Agencies such as W.H.O., F.A.O. and Unesco. There is no reason to denigrate the activities of these bodies. They are valuable and promising as far as they go. The complaint is that they do not go far enough and they need therefore to be reviewed and supplemented from other sources. They need more first-class servants; at present they are a mixture of the first-class and the superannuated or unwanted. They need to be co-ordinated, and in particular the central organs of the U.N. need firmer control over the Specialized Agencies, which were established by the Charter as autonomous bodies and have become more rather than less independent as they have expanded. But probably the most important reform concerns the most important figure, the man on the spot, the resident representative of the U.N. for technical aid. Within his restricted field of advice and provision, he is a key figure in the struggle to endow weaker states with prosperity and coherence.

The usual questions about aid read like an extract from a grammar: to whom, by whom, how, why, how much? These questions obscure, because they by-pass, one significant element in the attempt to give stability to new states. The basic weakness of these states is the paucity of people who know their job. Now, the best way to get to know your job is to talk shop, and if you want a state to be better run, one of the best ways is to send its politicians, civil servants, judges, journalists, and other responsible professional persons to conferences attended by politicians, civil servants, judges, journalists, and other responsible persons from other countries.[1] There is no better way

[1] The conferences, seminars and exchanges in newspaper columns and newspaper offices across frontiers which have been organized by the International Press Institute have been one of the more notable, if less noted, contributions to international concord in the last decade.

of educating politicians in the business of being efficient at politics than to give them a chance to discuss common problems with other politicians; ministers will discuss ways of fending off backbenchers and backbenchers will exchange stories about how to get the better of ministers. Similarly civil servants will learn far more from each other than they can learn from ministers or vice versa. All over the world politicians need educating, for it is useless to extol parliamentary democracy without ensuring an adequate supply of reputable parliamentarians. The need for professional interchanges is no less great in the legal profession. The judiciary is the outward sign of the rule of law and the magistrate its most vital guardian, for the man who believes that his neighbour owes him ten shillings has the choice between going to a court for redress and taking the law into his own hands by setting upon his neighbour. In most states the judicial machinery and the habit of resorting to it are both dangerously weak. The judicature has to establish by efficiency and rectitude that it is better to go to law than to go berserk. This is no easy task for a small group of men in a new state, and their determination may be strengthened and their effectiveness reinforced by contacts with their fellows who have the good fortune to practise law where law is taken for granted.

III

Foreign aid may help to stabilize a state. Some kinds of aid are specially helpful, though their products may not always be so benign as teachers, doctors and engineers. I have in mind aid given to the strong arm of the law and to armies.

Mr. Nehru is known to have grudged every penny spent on the Indian army, and Mr. Nyerere has said that what Tanganyika needs is not an army but a police force. But many of the new states are born with armies and the rest will acquire them. The benevolent outsider will wish these armies to play a constructive role within the state and none save a deterrent role in its external relations. At present no African state is capable of mounting an invasion of a neighbouring country on a scale significant by the standards of other continents, nor do the various territorial disputes to be found within Africa seem likely to produce ungovernable trouble in the immediate future. But the general meagreness of African forces is not in itself a guarantee of peace, for it can be argued that the higher the level of force, the stronger its deterrent effect. Moreover, Africa can hardly hope to escape boundary disputes and tensions of the kind which normally induce national leaders to spend more and more on armaments. An arms race in Africa is therefore a serious possibility. President Eisenhower spoke warningly of it at the U.N. General Assembly in September 1960, and the British as well as the Americans have toyed with the idea of rationing the supply of arms to Africa by international agreement.

Plans of this kind recall the nineteenth century, when peace was kept in Africa by the principal powers which divided the continent into spheres of influence and tried to operate an embargo on arms, but the latter part of the programme was only moderately successful, and the prospects for any such embargo in the twentieth century are exceedingly remote. Arms have been plentiful and easy to come by since the end of the second World War and the dispersion of what the British left behind in the Suez base. Except in relation to nuclear weapons (where there is already a tacit embargo on supply, even to allies), no international agreement limiting supplies of arms to other countries is likely outside a general disarmament convention. The Russians offered to negotiate an agreement of this kind in relation to Asia and Africa in 1956 and again in 1960, but their reasons may well have been purely tactical (to stop the supply of Western arms to the friends of the West), and any agreement of this kind would seem to run counter to the Moscow declaration of Communist parties of December 1960. An agreement between the principal arms-producing governments to regulate in concert the supply of arms to other countries would diminish the chances for mischief in the world, but a total embargo is neither practical at present nor clearly desirable.

From the practical point of view an embargo on the supply of heavy arms such as aircraft, submarines and tanks is possible. It is also well worth while, since these weapons are specially offensive and unstabilizing, and a Western initiative to limit and control their supply would be a useful contribution to peace—and to the budgets of new states.[1] Attempts to stop the traffic in smaller weapons, however, would run up against very great obstacles. Widespread agreement would be necessary, including the agreement of minor producers, and in order to make the ban effective it would be necessary to create machinery to spot and stop evasions; the U.N. commission in Laos failed to keep foreign arms out of that country. An embargo would almost certainly induce non-producers to engage in the under-cover traffic in arms or to start producing themselves at ruinous expense or to go shopping for arms in Communist countries (as the Republicans had to in the Spanish Civil War, to the great advantage of the hitherto insignificant Communist group among them, when the British and French governments refused to supply them in the name of non-intervention.) In any case, the result would be less local stability and not more. Moreover, states have legitimate uses for arms for their own internal security, and in new states with a defective consensus of feeling in favour of law and order this need for military and police force is greater than in, say, Britain. Indonesia provides an excellent example of the risks at either end of the scale. If the government is poorly equipped, the country lapses into chaos, but if it is well equipped it may feel tempted to attack Western New Guinea (Irian).

We must conclude that all but the smallest new states [2] will have arms and that the West will be asked to supply them and

[1] The distinction between offensive and defensive conventional weapons is becoming increasingly useful, since at this level defensive weapons are steadily gaining over offensive weapons technologically and tactically, e.g. anti-tank and anti-aircraft guided weapons over tanks and aircraft.

[2] Perhaps Sierra Leone with a population of $2\frac{1}{4}$ million will decide to do without an army (at an annual cost of £1 million per battalion) if it has a police force capable of dealing with the occasional diamond riot.

will find it inexpedient to refuse. Of what sort will these armies be? And can the West influence their development? Liberal democracies have an anti-military bias; they insist on the separation of the civil and military power even more than they insist on the mutual independence of legislature, judiciary and executive. The trespass of a military man into the civil sphere is regarded as a sign of ill health, and this doctrine derived from Western history and traditions has been reinforced by observing the fortunes of other parts of the world, notably Latin America, where military castes have misgoverned country after country and have raised armies incapable of doing anything except overturn governments. The same could happen in Africa but it need not. That African armies will acquire power and influence in African states is likely; that they will abuse their position need not be assumed.

It is related of Professor Yadin, who was Chief of Staff of the Israeli Army at the age of 31, that having served in that office until he was 35 he resigned and advised Mr. Ben-Gurion never to allow any individual to hold the highest military post in so small a country for more than three years, lest the army acquire an unhealthy dominance. Not all military chiefs are so self-effacing, and experience has shown the proneness of new states (among others) to fall under military rule. Egypt, Pakistan, Burma and the Sudan have welcomed generals who promised reforms or efficiency or honesty and many a general or colonel is tempted to think of himself as the saviour with the sword even if it is not too clear what needs to be saved. In Africa even Nigeria, vast but loose, could be dominated by an army of one division with a few helicopters and some modern signals equipment. Senegal and Mali have inherited strong military traditions and institutions from France. Other countries have nuclei.

In composite states like Nigeria and Ghana the army may reflect local rivalries and so accentuate inherent instabilities. Thus in Ghana a large proportion of the officers comes from the south. Some say that this is political favouritism, others that it reflects the better education of the south; both explanations could be true, but neither will dispel the dissatisfaction of northerners, who feel that they are not getting their fair share of places in an honoured and well paid profession. In the Sudan a similar unbalance to the detriment of the south is being alleviated. This is but one example of how an army can promote instability, and there are others, such as the disruption of an army by competing loyalties or bribes, as in the Congo.

But an army can also play an exactly opposite role. We may refer again to Israel—if, however, with the proviso that the smallness of the country and its European traditions enabled it to create a citizen army on the Swiss model. In both these respects Israel is exceptional, and any analogy with other new states, especially the larger African ones, needs to be drawn with more than ordinary caution. In Israel the army is the principal formative and cohesive power in the State. It instils into its recruits that feeling of nationhood, of belonging, without which a community can easily fall apart. If at the same time it fosters an anxious nationalism, it also offsets this volatile emotion by training men in modern skills and so turning them towards the love of ordered progress and study which is characteristic of the professional class and is one of the most pacific forces in any society. To the military concept of law and order is added the law-abiding orderliness of the middle classes, who mind going to prison and dislike destruction. What has been done in Israel may be attempted in Africa too. In Nigeria (although the Ibos by reason of their education provide a disproportionate number of officers and so excite the jealousy of other races) the army claims to be a cohesive and not a disruptive force, because no units are recruited regionally and all move from one part of the Federation to another; they have no regional loyalties. In this respect the Nigerian government is consciously or unconsciously following an example set by Marshal Tito when the new federal Yugoslav state and army were formed after the last war.

Outsiders can contribute to the cultivation of the more estimable qualities of armed forces. Colonial and ex-colonial powers in particular have links which need to be refashioned rather than broken. The training which they have given in the past and continue to give today should be extended as far as possible; where they used to instruct subordinates, they may now help friends. In the military sphere they can do three things. They can train junior officers and N.C.O.s, they can train staff officers, and they can send advisory missions overseas. The last of these three methods is the best for people in a hurry, but in the longer term the opening of course to foreigners is more fruitful and the training of younger men preferable to the training of their seniors—on the principle adopted by such diverse bodies as the Jesuits and the British Council of catching them young. Staff officers attended the appropriate courses at the Staff Colleges in Britain,[1] although there is no gainsaying the fact that candidates from many overseas countries are often markedly, if not surprisingly, less well qualified than British officers of equal rank and therefore less well able to stay the course. And the more who come, the more will this be so, with the result that candidates will be encouraged to enter upon training for which many of them may be unqualified; there is a danger of letting goodwill outrun good sense. There has been some discussion about special one-year courses for overseas candidates, but unfortunately any such courses are bound to be regarded as inferior to the real thing and a way of fobbing off foreigners with second-rate instruction and concealing the latest gadgets from them. Security has not so far proved a serious obstacle, and few complaints are made against the current practice whereby foreigners are required to leave staff courses before the end (American and Commonwealth officers being excluded from one small exercise only).

For junior officers there is a wide range of possibilities. Besides courses at the Staff Colleges there are over two hundred other courses run by the British Army and open to foreigners [2] and as many again run by the Navy and the Air Force. These

[1] Thirty-one foreign and Commonwealth officers attended the Army Staff College in Britain in 1961 and the number will be greater in 1962. At the Royal Military College, where there is considerable pressure on space, about 170 places are allotted to cadets from foreign and Commonwealth countries. The R.A.F. Staff College has a special wing for training foreign officers alongside British officers.

[2] In 1960–1 1,682 officers, officer cadets and other ranks from forty-six countries attended these army courses.

courses are mainly technical. In addition Britain is at present engaged in a new experiment. A conference on defence administration was assembled in the autumn of 1961 to discover whether there is a corpus of knowledge on defence administration which is required by all and sundry. The conference, which was open to and attended by officers from old and new states from every continent, may lead to the creation of a British or International College of Defence Administration.

The principal object of the internationalization of military knowledge and ideas is to foster professional efficiency. If armies are to be important, they had better be efficient. Their officers, whether they remain soldiers or become one day soldier-presidents, should also imbibe the standards of personal integrity which have been a hall-mark of the military caste in many Western countries. Beyond that Western military instructors will not go. In Britain above all it would be repugnant to the military mind to become involved in the dissemination of political ideas, and the notion of using staff courses for cold war propaganda would send a cold shiver down every military spine. Nevertheless the West will gain some political advantage from giving technical assistance to foreign officers, if those officers learn by example to eschew the use of military power to overcome political shortcomings and *vice versa*, and if they imbibe a healthy theory of civil-military relations. The Russians are prevented from obtaining similar advantages because of their lack of a common language with Africans and their neuroses about security.

The ex-colonial powers are not the only countries which can provide the training that new countries seek. Other members of the Western alliance, notably the United States, and other members of the Commonwealth, such as Canada with its pronounced international leanings, can do so too; certain kinds of training can most readily be given in India and Pakistan, where climatic and political conditions are closer to those of most new states than are Britain's. African forces are likely to have to cope with situations that are familiar to Indians and Pakistanis, but no longer exercise the minds and weapons of British officers at home. The Commonwealth is experimenting with schemes for mutual assistance in education, medicine, etc.; it could do something similar for military science.

But the analogy is not exact. Education and medicine are unexceptionable processes. Military activities are suspect and the rulers of new states are not free to accept military technical aid in the same way as they may accept other kinds of aid. An African Commonwealth Prime Minister will fear the reproaches of other Afro-Asians and of the opposition in his own country if he associates himself with anything that could be dubbed neo-colonialism. Hence, for example, the dismissal by President Nkrumah of General Alexander, almost certainly a sop to internal opposition. It would therefore be a mistake to give military aid a formal superstructure; institutions are easier to attack, and more difficult to enter into, than activities. The Commonwealth's contribution should take the form of a network of bilateral exchanges, of which the presence in Ghana of an Indian air mission and Canadian army officers has been a useful prototype.

The Western tradition draws a sharp distinction between army and police functions. The army, it is held, is not the proper instrument for keeping order. That is a job for the police, and it is important that soldiers should not be regarded as fit for police duties simply because they wear uniforms; in fact, they are not trained for police duties and are often baffled or resentful when called upon to perform them. If the police fail, then the army may be called upon to restore order—which is something quite different. Moreover, the most that the army can do is to recapture control of a situation and then turn it over again to the police. The use of military troops is in any case a hazardous one, since their employment too early or to excess, while effective in restoring order on the surface, may aggravate the underlying problem. It follows that, if the distinction between the two roles is to be observed, a state must have an efficient police force as well as an efficient army.

Police forces are of three kinds. In relatively settled communities they derive their effectiveness from the confidence of the public. In less stable countries and in colonial territories, where government is by authority and not consent, they depend upon the rulers. Finally, there is the so-called police state in which they are an essential element in government, but are trusted neither by public nor by rulers. With this third kind of police we are not here concerned.

In dependent territories it is, or should be, a principal concern of government to convert the police force from the second to the first of these categories by independence day at the latest, and secondly to instil the lesson (without which the principal task cannot be achieved) that a police force is not an instrument to be used for political purposes. Rulers in new states, straining against odds to achieve great things in next to no time, are inevitably tempted to use methods which are obnoxious in countries where these things have already been achieved, and particularly to attain by the use of power objectives which they do not hope to reach by persuasion without intolerable delay.[1] The use of the police in this context is very convenient, and it is, to take a single example, a tribute both to President Nkrumah and to the police mission sent by Britain to the colony of the Gold Coast that the Ghanaian police has been open to so little criticism since independence.[2] The final service that a colonial power can render a dependent territory at the time of change is not to denude the territory of its police by offering immediately tempting terms for retirement. Malaya, which had been equipped with an excellent police force, was handicapped in this way, and some of the departing officers themselves soon found that they were being employed in new and inappropriate jobs where their talents were being wasted.

The adequacy of a police force is not measured by its size. An

[1] There is a parallel here between the ambitions of new rulers in Africa and the reforming Sultans in nineteenth century Turkey who felt obliged to increase their despotic powers in order to put through their programmes. Atatürk, the great modernizer, followed the same autocratic path.

[2] After independence new states may get from abroad aid in police matters on the same sort of basis as technical military aid. In Britain the Police College at Bramshill has a few places for overseas officers, and technical training centres, such as Scotland Yard, also open their doors to foreigners. For special purposes advisory missions are sent to countries which ask for them.

adequate police force is one that fulfils a variety of conditions. Colonial powers have discovered by trial and error what these conditions are, and although the colonial period is now over, the lessons the colonial powers have learnt are worth transcribing, since the problems have not been wafted away with them. In the first place a police force must recruit men of the right sort. In multi-racial or multi-religious societies the force should likewise be mixed. The police must not be exposed to the stresses of divided loyalties which may cause the force to melt away in an emergency—as happened on occasions in Malaya and Cyprus (although in India loyalty to the Raj over-rode communal loyalties until the British made known their intention to withdraw almost at once). It should not, like the Force Publique in the Congo, be officered by a special caste, in that case by aliens. It should be seen to be something different from the army; policemen should not be regarded as soldiers wearing a different uniform, though the distinction is not easily drawn if the local language, Swahili for example, has only one word for both. The Special Branch, whose business it is to keep authority well informed, should never be neglected and should constantly bear in mind one of the first principles of police (learnt in the tough period from Fielding to Peel when the British police was being invented), that the police must make and keep contact with the forces of disorder in order to be able to catch and defeat them and so earn the gratitude and co-operation of the silent mass of the community.

IV

I have set down certain things about the older and more established states, and some other things about their newer and less firm brethren, which are relevant to the problem of achieving peace between nations. The general conclusion must be that peace is a precarious and intermittent boon. So long as the task of keeping nations at peace is left to the nations individually, there is not much reason to expect that they will often be successful. Achieving peace between nations requires collaboration between nations to that end. But before we turn to the capacities and potentialities of the U.N. we should consider for a moment an intermediate form of political activity, namely action by a regional group of states which is smaller than the total society of nations. In this category I do not include alliances like Nato, Cento, Seato, Anzus or the Warsaw Pact, but I have in mind ostensibly more permanent groups whose professed first aim is to keep the peace within a given area. While alliances such as Nato are formed with an eye to an outside enemy, these other regional groups look inward rather than outward. Two of them—the Arab League and the embryonic African High Command—have arisen as expressions of local solidarity in areas from which alien dominance is being withdrawn. A third—the Organization of American States—is a miniature, territorially delimited, league of nations, created in order to promote the pacific settlement of inter-state disputes within its area and endowed with machinery for setting force in motion against an aggressor. The basis of all these groups is a pledge by each member to regard aggression against one as aggression against all. What follows in their various constitutions differs, but in no case are the members prepared to promise in advance much more than consultation. They pledge their attitudes, but not, save within harmless limits, their actions. They fit into the U.N. scheme of things, since the U.N. Charter makes explicit provision for the establishment of regional groups, and there was in the period of the U.N.'s gestation a school of thought which advocated the creation of strong regional groups surmounted by a less obtrusive oecumenical superstructure. If this conception had prevailed, power —and with it the primary responsibility for keeping peace *in suo orbe*—would have resided with the group rather than with the overall council or assembly, but a different distribution of powers was adopted and the regional groups have been animated not by the Charter but by local circumstances. For practical purposes they exist independently of the U.N., even it sometimes seems despite the U.N. Yet they may come to have a part to play in peace-keeping, and in theory a regional body capable of a measure of local policing would relieve the U.N. of part of its burden.

A regional group may serve to keep the peace precisely because it is a sublimation of the sort of local feeling which, in the form of nationalism, is a fruitful source of war. A regional group combines the nationalist passions for keeping others out and running one's own affairs, with an expressed purpose to settle disputes between nations by peaceful means. Thus the embryonic African High Command is an attempt to secure for Africans a prior right and adequate power to cope with disorder in Africa, but in order to justify itself it must, in fact, keep peace not merely that alien powers may be kept out but also that the U.N. may be spared the occasion to intervene.

The African High Command is (in 1961) a tenuous affair. It emerged out of tentative plans first sketched during 1960 in Cairo and Accra at a time when African leaders were becoming dissatisfied with the U.N.'s attitude in the Congo and were turning their minds to the possibility of a joint African expedition, distinct from the U.N. force, in order to prevent the secession of Katanga. In December President Nkrumah threatened the withdrawal of the Ghanaian and other African contingents and the formation of an African High Command if the U.N. failed to secure the immediate release of Mr. Lumumba, the evacuation of all Belgian troops, and the disarming of Colonel Mobutu's units and other particularist forces. In January 1961 five African states (the United Arab Republic, Morocco, Ghana, Guinea and Mali),[1] with representatives of the Algerian revolutionary government and Ceylon, met in conference at Casablanca and declared their intention of withdrawing from the Congo and of forming an African High Command and consultative assembly. President Nkrumah said that the Casablanca group was determined to build a strong union of African states. The conference brought together two separate trends: dissatisfaction with developments in the Congo and a wider panafricanism which was quite distinct from the particular Congo problem but was hardly less interventionist in

[1] Lybia sometimes looked like a sixth member of this group, sometimes not.

temper. Four months later President Nasser was talking of an
African charter to be signed in the first instance by the six
independent African members of the Casablanca group and of
the emergence of the promised High Command by July, to be
followed by the establishment of economic and cultural com-
mittees and a meeting of Foreign Ministers in September.

These groupings had meanwhile conduced to the formation
of a separate and increasingly rival African group, formed at
Brazzaville by twelve French-speaking states (to which others,
such as Nigeria, Sierra Leone, Liberia, Tunisia, Ethiopia and
Somalia, have loosely attached themselves at various times).
This Brazzaville group, whose leading members were Senegal
and the Ivory Coast, had first come together in October 1960
to discuss the Algerian question. The emphasis at the Brazzaville conference of December 1960, and the wider Monrovia
conference of May 1961, was on economic and political co-
operation of a limited kind; their resolutions reflected the particular cruxes of the moment (Algeria, atom bomb tests in Africa,
apartheid, Angola) rather than any real will to form a durable
and effective union. The emergence of this group was not a
move towards a regional supervision of African affairs, but
rather the opposite, since the numerically superior Brazzaville
group could prevent the more determined but sparser Casablanca group from creating any organization which could
justly claim to speak for Africa. On the other hand, the Casablanca group had the advantage in personalities (Presidents
Nasser and Nkrumah outshone every leader in the other
group) and in the supply of arms (rifles, automatic weapons
and ammunition are manufactured in Egypt).

The Arab League, which was formed with British prompting
in 1945, has waxed and waned with the fortunes of panarabism.
It has had its moments, serving for example as the vehicle for
the reconciliation of the United Arab Republic and Jordan in
1959, but it has been powerless to prevent the waging of hot
and cold war in the Middle East and has been driven to the
point of ridicule by the mutual jealousies and antagonisms of
its larger members. It played a significant part in getting the
Americans and the British out of Lebanon and Jordan after the

adventures of July 1958, but for the most part it has been fully occupied preserving its unity or concealing its disunity, and its attempts to create an effective mutual defence system have failed. Its failures have not all been of its own making, for the British, having sponsored the League, refused in the fifties to let it become the basis for a Middle East defence system and disrupted both the League and the Middle East by the abrupt change of policy signalized by the Baghdad Pact—that huge error which negated the new start in Anglo-Egyptian relations and, by adopting an Iraqi-centred policy, aggravated inter-Arab tensions and opened the door to Russian influence in the Middle East.

The Arab League is ostensibly a racial rather than a regional group, but before the admission of Tunisia and Morocco it was, in fact, also a regional group. It cannot function as a group, however, so long as the chief political characteristic of the race or the region is disunity. The Arab League may be a part of the advance guard of panarabism and panarabism may prove a pacifying force, but the League's present incapacity was displayed at the time when this book was being written. Iraq claimed, and seemed to be about to take, possession of Kuwait. No other Arab state wanted this to happen, but the decisive action was taken not by any one of them, nor by the Arab League, but by the British, who in effect occupied the sheikhdom by a well timed, painless and economical *coup* in order to preserve it from a fate equivalent to death. The League later retrieved its reputation and replaced the British (who were very willing to go), but the dissolution of the United Arab Republic almost immediately winded it once more. It has often been said that the Israeli problem keeps the League in being, but no league is necessary to unite Arabs over Israel, and the League's chief functions at the present time are to demonstrate the ineffectiveness of a regional group in a disharmonious region and to try to survive into more harmonious times.

The Organization of American States is a regional group with a difference. Its basis is severely geographical. Although nearly all its members are Spanish by tongue, the existence of one Portuguese-, one French- and one English-speaking member deprives it of any semblance of embodying hispanidad as the Arab League claims to embody panarabism. The organization was created by a treaty signed at Petropolis near Rio de Janeiro in December 1947, and endowed with a charter at the ninth International Conference of American States, held at Bogota in April 1948. The idea of inter-American co-operation is, however, much older, and the pledge to regard aggression against one as aggression against all had been taken at Havana in 1940 and repeated at Chapultepec in 1945. After the war all the American states except Canada and, initially, Nicaragua joined the new organization. While envisaging the use of armed forces to prevent or stop aggression in the hemisphere, they stipulated that no state should be required to use it in a particular case against its own will. Argentina wished to limit the obligations to instances of aggression from outside the hemisphere, but this proposal was defeated. Another Argentinian proposal requiring unanimity before collective action was also defeated in favour of a two-thirds rule. Aggression was expressly extended to cover acts which did not amount to armed aggression.

The charter of the organization enunciated a number of principles (including the principle of non-interference in the domestic affairs of a state) and created certain permanent organs (a quinquennial conference, ad hoc meetings of Foreign Ministers, a council of ambassadorial status, a secretariat called the Pan-American Union and two specialized institutions). The Bogota conference also adopted a series of treaties and resolutions, including a resolution concerning the defence of democracy in America. There was already apparent at this conference a conflict between political purposes of this kind, which became increasingly important in Washington's eyes, and the concern of the great majority of other members with economic problems in priority to military co-operation and ideological apprehensions. Latin America believed that Washington could best exorcize Communism and civil disorders by helping to raise Latin American standards of living.

The organization's first test came soon after the Bogota conference. Costa Rica and Nicaragua were on bad terms and each harboured within its territory malcontents from across their common frontier. A presidential election in Costa Rica in February 1948 was followed by a short civil war and then at the end of the year the defeated party launched an invasion from Nicaragua. Costa Rica invoked the treaty of 1947 and the Council of the Organization promptly despatched a commission of five to go and find out what was really happening. The commission arrived on the scene within a week of the original appeal and produced a report which blamed Nicaragua for allowing, if not encouraging, the invasion. The council called for a cease-fire and persuaded the two neighbours to sign a treaty of friendship.

The friendship was, however, not real and the situation repeated itself in January 1955. Once again the council held an emergency session and sent a commission of inquiry to investigate a Costa Rican complaint of imminent invasion. The commission's anti-Nicaraguan findings induced the council to call for help for Costa Rica, which was promptly supplied with a few aircraft by the United States. A buffer zone was established, the rebels withdrew, the quarrel sank below the surface, fresh agreements were signed by the two states and the O.A.S. reaped good opinions for the promptness and usefulness of its actions. Later in the year it intervened when Ecuador found itself menaced by Peru by land and sea, and again the danger of conflict evaporated.

These conflicts involved no major powers and raised no major issues. In Guatemala it was different. Guatemala, which had been ruled by a dictatorship from 1930 to 1944, was a country where wealth and power were in the hands of a very few. Moreover, the preponderant economic influence was foreign, that of the United Fruit Company. President Arbenz, who was elected to that office in 1952, wanted to speed up economic and social reform and introduced certain measures which made him very unpopular with neighbouring governments (mindful of their own inadequacies) and in Washington. President Arbenz was not a Communist, but some of his supporters were, and it was convenient to call him one. At the tenth conference of American states in Caracas in March 1954 Mr.

Dulles tried to rouse Latin America against the Guatemaltecan régime by dilating upon the dangers of the growth of Communism in the continent. His attitude was ill conceived and the Guatemaltecan Foreign Minister received an ovation from the conference, which was ready enough to give oblique voice to anti-Yanqui feelings and was almost ready to see in President Arbenz (who was in this respect a forerunner of Fidel Castro) the champion of Latin America's ills. But the conference contended itself with this demonstration and allowed Mr. Dulles to have a resolution which, though watered down, was sufficiently to his liking to enable him to leave Caracas with some show of having accomplished his purpose.

After the conference tension in Central America increased. Guatemala's neighbours complained that it was exporting Communism, the United States tried to organize an embargo on the delivery of arms to Guatemala, and Guatemala applied successfully to Czechoslovakia for arms and complained to the Security Council of infringements of its frontiers with Honduras and Nicaragua. In June Guatemala was invaded from Honduras. At this point President Arbenz agreed to accept an O.A.S. mission of inquiry, but before it arrived he had been defeated and evicted. The American ambassador, who played an open and leading part in organizing the revolt against the President, was given credit for forestalling U.N. or O.A.S. intervention. Speed won.[1]

In the Cuban crisis in 1961 the O.A.S. was again left out of the picture. The issues raised by fidelismo probed the members in a tender spot and divided them, and the active intervention of the Organization's one over-mighty member paralysed it. The separate intervention of a major power, however inefficient, expunges the possibility of intervention by a regional group.

[1] I have heard it said that the State Department was innocent of intervention in Guatemala and that the American hand was, as in Cuba, that of the Central Intelligence Agency. I have been unable to arrive at the truth of the matter. Both versions of the story are odd.

Hungary is another example of a major power intervening in such a way that its will is done in a trice. Disorder has been eliminated before anybody else can set about eliminating it. The threat to peace has been liquidated—along with other things.

These three regional groups do not have a great deal in common, but certain generalizations are possible. None of them can be expected to intervene in a dispute between states of any substance. The most mature of them, the Organization of American States, can settle minor inter-American disputes, but it played no part—or a merely formal and perfunctory part—in the Guatemaltecan and Cuban affairs which involved the United States. The Arab League is reduced to impotence in every phase of the Iraqi-Egyptian dispute, and it is hardly conceivable that an Asian group, if there had been one, would have been allowed to intervene in Kashmir; where states of the calibre of India and Pakistan are embroiled, only the U.N. can step in. But in marginal areas, away from the centres of cold war, regional groups could play a useful role and save other people a lot of trouble. The rest of the world would be only too pleased if the Arab League were capable of imposing peace with justice round Kuwait, or—to take a problematic example —if possible trouble in the Cameroons could be left to Nigeria and one or two other West African states. There are bound to be emergencies in which action by the U.N. or by a major power or alliance is ruled out for some reason or other, and a regional group which stepped into the gap would not only be performing a vital service but would also be giving its members practical training in the techniques and doctrines of responsible collective action.

As a corollary we may propound a second generalization to the effect that any regional group which includes one of the major powers, or which trespasses into the cold war, is more likely to be used than useful. The United States has on occasion shown signs of wanting to turn the O.A.S. into an anti-Communist body, and it is reasonable to suppose that the Russians dream of turning it into an anti-American body. The Arab League and an African High Command can easily become the objects of similar ambitions.

Thirdly, none of these groups can make war, if only because their members would never agree on any particular aggressive project. It may seem at first sight that the Arabs might combine against Israel and the Africans against the Union of South Africa, but even these ventures seem improbable. Regional groups are therefore probably unwarlike, if not necessarily peaceful.

Fourthly, they are by their very nature centripetal and foster the sense of belonging, which is a stabilizing factor. The pan-arab and panafrican creeds of Presidents Nasser and Nkrumah have been unjustly reviled by enemies determined to find nothing but evil in the ambitions of these leaders. Morally neutral, these creeds could be politically fruitful. But the analogy can easily be overdone. Panarabism is a much more precise force than panafricanism, for Africa is immensely larger than the Arab world and lacks the latter's linguistic, religious and ethnic unity.

But, finally, a comparison between these three groups leads one to conclude that a group of sovereign states co-operating within a settled geographical sphere is much more likely to be effective in the world today than a group which has been called into existence to assert and embody a non-existent or tenuous unity. An Arab group and an African group may, like the American group, contribute to the maintenance of peace within its orbit, but it is much less likely to do so if its inspiration is a panarabism or a panafricanism which does not correspond to any present political reality. The Arabs and the Africans do not even have a common view about outsiders (except that they should stay outside) and are no nearer to unity among themselves than the notoriously fissiparous Europeans. Their search for common ground may be held to them for merit. There is nothing ignoble about it; rather the reverse. But if it is directed to a unitary or even federal goal, it is almost certainly a quest for the unattainable and so a diversion from what is practical and valuable. We have seen the rise and evaporation of pan-slav, panislamic, panturanian and other agglomerative notions. They have not helped to keep the peace. Nor has Communism, the widest asseveration of them all. Every disorder begins somewhere. It is local, and organizations designed to avert or extinguish disorder should themselves be defined in hard geographical terms and not in visionary and provocative ideas. A regional group for keeping the peace should be an association of neighbours and neither explicitly nor implicitly a declaration of racial, religious or political principles.

Chapter 4

The United Nations

O F the motives which have contributed to the creation of an international organization in the present century the chief has been the desire to keep the peace. There was a time when keeping the peace was a comparatively unimportant matter. A government might seek peace or it might seek war, but the outcome of its endeavours was not the universal calamity which has become possible since science converted war into something so much more voracious than the professional occupation of soldiery. At the same time as war has become appalling, peace has become ever more intractable; scepticism has grown about the ability of national governments to prevent war, even when they wish to. Hence the revival of dormant schemes for an international authority which, whether by mediation or compulsion, might help to keep the peace.

The U.N. was endowed with this function at birth, charged by the first article of its Charter to suppress 'acts of aggression or other breaches of the peace' and permitted (article 42) itself to use force for this purpose and even in certain cases (chapter VII and article 2 (7)) to intervene in the internal affairs of a member state.

It is useless to discuss whether the organization's performance has been encouraging or disappointing, for a judgement on this issue is no more than a statement about the original expectations of the person making the judgement. Certain things have not been done, while others have. Some of the plans laid by the founders have miscarried, while developments not dreamt of in 1945 have come to pass. These we will briefly chronicle before proceeding to discuss practicable possibilities for reinforcing the U.N.'s peace-keeping capacities. But first let us permit ourselves a few generalizations.

Nobody in the world can seriously believe that the existence

of the U.N. guarantees peace. Nobody would have been justified in cherishing so extravagant a notion within seventeen
years of the end of the second World War, but the first basic
fact about the U.N. today is that the organization remains
fragile, ancillary and problematic; even about its survival, let
alone its efficiency, there is some doubt. Great numbers of
people rest their hopes upon it, but these hopes are not a reflection of faith so much as an appalled appreciation of the possibility of their hopes being misplaced. The U.N. may or may
not be able to perform its primary task. On this point there is
doubt. But there is less doubt about the consequences of its
failure. To take only one example: the future history of Africa
is so closely bound up with the U.N. that, although it is impossible to predict the course of events in that continent, it is
possible to assert that the course will be quite different if there
is an effective international organization and if there is not.

This awareness of the crucial importance of preserving and
strengthening an international authority is one of the U.N.'s
assets. A second is the fact that it has the confidence of the new
and the non-aligned states, who look to it not merely as a convenient platform for airing views, displaying personalities and
prosecuting national interests, but also as a source of justice and
order. So long as the U.N. is so regarded, some of the inevitable
conflicts between these states will be contained within its political organs and diverted into diplomatic channels. National
leaders know this and prize the U.N. accordingly.

A third asset of great price is the support of the United States.
I am not referring to the fact that the United States pays a large
part of the organization's expenses, for this circumstance is a
mixed blessing entailing the risk that the U.N. may be repre-
sented as an American vassal. (We shall come to finance later.)
I have in mind the widespread and genuine support for the
U.N. throughout the United States. At one time anti-U.N.
lobbies had either disappeared or been reduced to insignificance
and this popular support is all the more valuable since it is
parallelled in none of the other major states which have been
designated permanent members of the Security Council. Unfortunately, however, there are beginning to be signs of a less

enthusiastic attitude and there is some reason to fear a new and more hostile trend of opinion, especially if the Assembly votes in favour of recognizing the Peking government as the government of China.

Against these considerable assets are certain considerable liabilities. The first of these is the death of Mr. Hammarskjöld, a pioneer of amazing intellect, integrity and courage, of whom it can be said—as perhaps only of Pericles in the whole course of history—that when he died mankind faltered. Without departing from the letter of the Charter, Mr. Hammarskjöld used his powers to an effect not envisaged by the U.N.'s founding fathers.[1] In doing so he advanced the U.N. from infancy to adolescence, but at the same time he roused the distrust of adults, and with his death it may become easier for the adults to keep the adolescent in its place or even to push it back into pristine impotence.

The principal threat comes from the U.S.S.R. Mr. Hammarskjöld made explicit his view that the U.N. existed to help the majority of minor powers and not to serve the minority of major ones.[2] He also went some way to make the U.N. a political force independent of the entrenched privileges of the permanent members of the Security Council. Although the Americans did not demur at this development, the Russians, with some show of constitutional justification, did. They launched a personal attack on Mr. Hammarskjöld and a more general attack against his office, with the apparent intention of forcing Mr. Hammarskjöld to resign and of obstructing the installation of any successor. But Mr. Hammarskjöld, taking his stand upon his duty to the majority of his employers, refused to go, and the Russian proposal to put his office into commission found no

[1] But see his introduction to the *U.N. Annual Report 1961*, in which he argued that the framers of the Charter clearly envisaged an activist and not a quietist organization. Even though they may not have envisaged the kind of action taken fifteen years later, these actions could on this view be regarded as complying with the spirit as well as the letter of the Charter.

[2] See in particular his speech at Oxford on May 30th, 1961, published under the title *The International Civil Servant in Law and in Fact* (Oxford, The Clarendon Press, 1961).

support outside the Communist world (nor universal support within it). The Russian proposal, whereby the Secretary-General would be replaced by a triad or troika of secretaries required to act unanimously or not at all, was presented as a design to ensure impartiality in the running of the U.N.'s affairs, but it seemed to most people to be calculated rather to hobble the organization (by giving a veto to each of three secretaries, one of whom would be openly a representative of the Communist block) and to give it a spurious neutrality more like the non-intervention of a eunuch than the properly regulated activity of an honest man of parts. Mr. Adoula opined at the Belgrade conference in September 1961 that if there had been a troika at New York in 1960 there would have been no intervention in the Congo by the U.N. But although the troika plan has fallen on stony ground, variants of it are likely to crop up and the Russians will presumably persist in their general policy of curbing the U.N.

Russian opposition is not unique. French and British attitudes towards the United Nations are not much more favourable, although they have in the nature of things less impact. The older European peoples, with a history and habit of doing what they think best without submitting to criticism, take a somewhat jaundiced view of an international organization where they are in a minority and where the majority spends too much time raking over their past misdeeds. More specifically and more forcefully, the British cannot forget Suez and the French judge the U.N. in terms of Algeria. The alacrity of the British in jumping to wrong conclusions about U.N. operations in Katanga in September 1961, and in airing tendentious criticisms of some of the personalities involved, are symtomatic of a mood which pervades much (though not all) of Western Europe and which no leading politician has attempted to dispel. It is difficult to assess the extent of this mood, but its existence in some of the maturer democracies, which might have been expected to give a lead in marshalling opinion at home and abroad in favour of international authority and order, is a weakness for the U.N.

Finally, the U.N. suffers from a weakness of a more general

kind. The organization has the task of applying the rule of law where no law is. It is trying to establish an international order in advance of, or *pari passu* with, the development of the law which the order must reflect. There is, of course, a body of public and private international law, but this corpus is neither sufficiently settled nor sufficiently extensive to provide the sort of base which, in a nation state, gives precision and authority and consent to the operations of those who have to keep the peace.[1] This is not the place for a treatise on international law, but it is relevant to insist on the difficulty of evolving international force in the service of international order so long as members of the U.N. are unable to check the rights and wrongs of a particular case against statute or precedent and lack time-honoured rules of procedure. They will remain reluctant to entrust force to an organization which may use it waywardly or in accordance with the unchecked propensities of a majority guided by the interests of the moment rather than established usages.

And this reluctance has been strengthened by recent events. The Congo crisis laid upon the U.N. an obligation to help a government to restore order and so—if the means were to be willed along with the end—to use such force as might be necessary, and in the discharge of the duties assigned to him by the Security Council and the Assembly Mr. Hammarskjöld developed the theory that the force should come mainly from countries near to the scene of action—in this case from African states rather than non-African ones. Now, enforcement is an altogether different operation from containment; enforcement requires more powers and more forces, and the states which are asked to accord these powers and provide these forces are parting with a significant degree of political initiative. In the Congo case non-Africans were in effect asked to trust the Secretary-General and a group of African states which, though they were neutral in the cold war, were naturally disposed to take side in Congolese politics. Most members of the U.N. responded

[1] Within the U.N. the Office of Legal Council, the Division of Legal Administration, and the Division for Codification of International Law concern themselves with these matters.

favourably because they trusted Mr. Hammarskjöld, but now Mr. Hammarskjöld is dead and it is at least likely that another time the doubts and the reluctance will be greater. Since it is vain to expect Mr. Hammarskjöld's successor to have Mr. Hammarskjöld's authority—at least for a time—the only way to overcome this weakness in the organization is to build up the belief that the U.N. can be relied upon to act steadily and judiciously. Which needs rules, experiment and time.

II

From this view of the potentialities of the U.N. towards the end of 1961 we must proceed to examine its past performance in keeping peace. Its methods have been various, but broadly speaking they fall into three main categories. In one important venture, the Korean war, the U.N. designated one of its members and charged that member, the United States, to implement U.N. resolutions. Control of the operations was devolved on the United States. In other cases, notably the Suez and Congo affairs, troops and other material have been borrowed from members for operations which have then been conducted and controlled from the U.N. headquarters in New York. Thirdly come cases, such as the intervention in Lebanon in 1958, where the U.N.'s own resources have sufficed.

The history of these operations begins with the failure to implement that part of the Charter which was supposed to endow the U.N. with a peace-keeping force. Pursuant to article 43 of the Charter a Military Staff Committee was set up and given the responsibility for the strategic direction of armed forces to be placed at the disposal of the Security Council. But no such forces ever were made available. The Committee discussed for years what sort of force should be created to enable the U.N. to be a policeman as well as a mediator and counsellor, but American and Russian views proved irreconcilable and the Committee gave up in despair in July 1948. Briefly, the United States wanted a large force of about 300,000 men, while the

Russians, whose attitude on this count was more or less acceptable to the other permanent members of the Security Council, argued that a much smaller force was all that was required, since there was no question of operations against any but small transgressors; the offences of the larger powers were patently immune. A second bone of contention was the Russian contention that the several national contributions to the force must be the same in size and composition, to which the United States opposed the more flexible notion that they should be comparable in effectiveness but disparate in nature. Further, the Russians objected to the stationing of any foreign contingent on the soil of any member and insisted on a stringent right to recall a contingent when its job was judged to be done. So nothing happened and no single agreement between the U.N. and a member state for the provision of force under these arrangements was ever signed.

At about the time when the Military Staff Committee acknowledged failure, the Secretary-General, Mr. Trygve Lie, advanced a modest proposal for the creation of a small, non-military Field Service of 300 men for transport, communications and guard duties, and also a Field Reserve Panel of 2,000 men who might be called on for observation and supervision duties with U.N. missions. These proposals arose out of the U.N.'s experiences in Palestine, where its chief mediator, Count Folke Bernadotte, had been assassinated and its operations were much bemused through lack of a clear idea of what was going on. The Secretary-General's plan was eventually adopted despite Russian opposition but, except on paper, little was done at this time to remedy the U.N.'s lack of an active arm and an intelligence system.

The failure to implement article 43 of the Charter had proceeded hand in hand with the general stultification of the Security Council. but during 1947 the Americans attempted to by-pass the Council and to revive the possibility of U.N. action by giving the General Assembly something of the competence originally reserved to the concert of Security Council Powers. At the opening of the 1947 Assembly, General Marshall proposed that the Assembly should in effect resolve to sit *en permanence* by creating an image of itself called the Interim Committee (or, more popularly, the Little Assembly). This proposal was adopted in November of that year and the Interim Committee existed, at first from year to year and later on an indefinite basis, until it ceased after 1950 to function except for a single annual meeting for the election of officers. Its authors justified its creation by reference to article 22 of the Charter, which authorizes the General Assembly to establish subsidiary organs, but the Russians and their associates denounced it as an attempt to circumvent the Charter and never attended any of its meetings. Consequently it was as impotent as the Military Staff Committee, and it is important only because its manifest ineffectiveness drove national leaders back into reliance on military alliances based on deterrence (if they had indeed ever thought of placing their faith in anything else) and away from all trust in collective security based on international law and sanctions.

This distressing disintegration was to some extent alleviated by some tentative, though promising, ventures in the techniques of observation and conciliation and was then momentarily, if illusorily, arrested by the great venture in enforcement in Korea. It is convenient to deal first with the Korean expedition of 1950–1, even though it followed the less spectacular missions sent in 1947–9 to Greece, Kashmir and Palestine.

On June 25th 1950 the U.N. commission on Korea (UNCOK), which had been established to try to effect the re-unification of that divided country and had additionally been charged to observe and report on anything likely to lead to a military clash, reported that South Korea had been invaded by the North Koreans. A war, capable of turning into a major conflict, was started. The United Nations promptly intervened. The action of President Truman, who gave the lead and provided most of the sinews, was widely acclaimed as an act of statesmanship which had saved the U.N. from declining into ineptitude like the League of Nations. The U.N. was doing the most difficult of all the things it was supposed to do, the one thing that the League had never done. Yet the U.N. intervention in Korea was a freak, for it was made possible only by the absence of the

U.S.S.R. from the Security Council for reasons that had nothing to do with Korea—still something of a mystery and perhaps Stalin's biggest blunder. Moreover, as the war proceeded, the Chinese joined in and the U.N.'s collective security crusade became in effect a war between two major powers, the United States and China. At this point the business of rectifying a breach of international law and order was subordinated to stopping a war that had become too dangerous, and President Truman's dismissal of General MacArthur, who was prepared to wage such a war, showed that international police action was not to be allowed to proceed to its conclusion if major powers were directly involved against one another.

There had nevertheless been a recrudescence of faith in collective action and the high tide was marked by a fresh attempt to give punch to the U.N. If the Korean venture had been but an eccentric accident, could not something be done to make future Koreas possible even in less extraordinary circumstances? In other words, to find a way of enabling the U.N. to do it again even if the Russians were in their place at the Security Council and unwilling to let the machinery be used? Once again the United States turned to the General Assembly.

The Uniting For Peace resolution, which was passed by the Assembly on November 3rd 1950, empowered the Assembly to consider any threat to peace which the Security Council failed to deal with; [1] provided for the convening of an emergency session of the Assembly at twenty-four hours' notice; created a Peace Observation Commission whose function was to get intelligence (but the Commission languished and lapsed); called on members to earmark armed contingents for service with the U.N.; and created a Collective Measures Committee to consider ways of strengthening peace. A fortnight later the Assembly also passed the Peace Through Deeds resolution, which called for prompt and united action against aggression and condemned attempts to subvert legally constituted governments by

[1] There must first be a veto in the Security Council. But it is possible to procure a veto either by forcing the Russian pace or by vetoing one's own resolution. The latter course has never been adopted so far.

interfering in their internal affairs. Thus the temper of the 1950 Assembly, the first to be held after the aggression in Korea, was ebullient.

Korea is the only place where the U.N. has ever intervened primarily in order to fight. Elsewhere its interventions have necessarily entailed readiness to be shot at, and in at least one case, the Congo, military activities were forced upon U.N. forces, but the more usual pattern of U.N. intervention has been investigation. This pattern was set as early as 1946, when the Greek Government complained of violations of its northern frontiers. Two commissions were successively dispatched to the area: the U.N. Commission of Investigation (UNCI) and the U.N. Special Committee on the Balkans (UNSCOB). The first was established by the Security Council in order to ascertain facts. It consisted of one representative of each member of the Security Council, together with a secretariat of twenty-seven. It was instructed to investigate by making inquiries of governments, officials and other individuals, to report and to make proposals. Eventually it reached a strength of 150 persons. It went to Greece, held ninety-one meetings, conducted thirty-three field investigations, heard 238 witnesses and collected enough evidence to fill three large volumes. By a majority of eight to three it concluded that Yugoslavia, and to a lesser extent Albania and Bulgaria, were supporting guerrilla warfare in Greece, and its proposals included a suggestion for the maintenance of a small commission in the troubled area. In October 1947 the Assembly created UNSCOB and sent observer teams to Greece which covered some 500 miles of the Greek frontier in groups of six. Prevented by Russian opposition from doing anything more drastic to supplement UNCI's report, the U.N. did at least persist in keeping itself and the world informed about what was going on.

Very shortly afterwards a commission of a different kind was established. The partition of India in 1947 was effected at the price of much slaughter and very bad relations between the successor states of India and Pakistan. In Kashmir acrimony and turbulence amounted to a danger of war. The Security Council established, in January 1948, a commission of five (U.N.

Commission on India and Pakistan—UNCIP) to try to secure a cease-fire and a plebiscite in the disputed territory. This commission did not succeed in getting to the area until the middle of the year, but it then took a leading part in securing a cease-fire from the first day of 1949 and helped to negotiate the truce line that was finally accepted by both sides in July of that year. Thereafter it maintained about forty observers whose presence and reports have helped to quarantine local incidents and who still remain in the area although the commission itself has been dissolved.

Palestine provides a third example of this kind of U.N. intervention in an area of hostilities. The end of the British mandate on May 15th 1948 was immediately followed by fighting between Arabs and Jews. A first truce of four weeks from June 28th was negotiated by Count Bernadotte acting at the behest of the Security Council and backed by a small corps of officers from the United States, France and Belgium, and a number of guards recruited partly from U.N. staff and partly in the United States. When fighting was resumed the Security Council adopted a strong resolution which proclaimed that the situation constituted a threat to peace within the meaning of article 39 of the Charter and threatened action to enforce the cease-fire if the combatants continued to fail to observe it; in this case there was a more distinct element of enforcement behind the roles of observation and conciliation that were almost exclusively characteristic of UNCI, UNSCOB and UNCIP. The second cease-fire, imposed with the help of this threat, was supervised by UNTSO (U.N. Truce Supervision Organization), a body which grew to a strength of 682, was destined to play an important role at the time of the Anglo-Franco-Israeli attack on Egypt in 1956 and remains in existence at the present day.

The commissions sent to Kashmir and Palestine were operations run by the Secretary-General with persons selected and dispatched by him, and they were in this respect unlike the commissions in the Balkans which were inter-governmental bodies whose members were nominated by governments asked to participate. This latter kind of commission has proved the less effectual since the members, chosen for geographical and ideological reasons, seldom have much interest in their task and tend to cancel each other out. They serve as a symbol of the world's concern, but not as much more.

Thus by 1950 the U.N.'s chartered peace-keeping machinery had not been assembled, but the organization had contrived all the same to take action of various kinds and of increasingly ambitious scope. If the most ambitious, the war in Korea, was to prove a dead end, the experience gained in Greece, Kashmir and Palestine was capable of fruitful development. The first half of the fifties did not add much to these experiences, but the second half produced severe tests in Egypt, Lebanon and Laos. These must be considered in some detail before we come to the supreme trial so far, the Congo.

At Suez two permanent members of the Security Council were directly involved and used their vetoes. The Israeli invasion of Egypt began on October 29th. The Security Council was summoned within a few hours and met on the morning of the 30th. Later in the day a cease-fire resolution was vetoed by Britain and France. Accordingly a special meeting of the Assembly was convened under the Uniting For Peace resolution. It began its debate on November 1st and its first resolution was passed during the ensuing night. This resolution called for an immediate cease-fire, the withdrawal of Israeli and Egyptian forces behind their frontiers, an embargo on the supply of military goods to the area and thereafter the immediate reopening of the Suez Canal. Further resolutions were adopted on November 4th, 5th and 7th, and by the end of the first week after the invasion the pattern of U.N. intervention was established. The first of these resolutions required the creation of a U.N. Emergency Force (UNEF). The second set up a U.N. command to 'secure and supervise the cessation of hostilities', appointed the Canadian Major-General E. L. M. Burns of UNTSO to be 'chief of the command' and authorized him to recruit officers from countries other than the five permanent members of the Security Council, and delegated a wide degree of authority to the Secretary-General who found himself in a much more central and commanding position than Mr. Trygve Lie had occupied during the Korean War. Whereas in Korea the United States had led and largely provided a fighting force commanded by an American General chosen by and reporting to the President of the United States, UNEF was primarily a non-fighting force, charged to prevent and not to win battles and controlled by the Secretary-General acting in concert with an advisory committee of representatives of seven medium powers [1] designated by the General Assembly. The Korean expedition was handed over to the United States by the U.N. and there was little that was international about it except its flag, a small proportion of the troops engaged, and possibly its conscience; Washington did not even accept the idea of an international advisory committee.[2] The Suez operation on the other hand was handled by the U.N. through its own organs, and the chain of command ran from the Secretary-General through the Commander of the Force to commanders of national units.

By November 7th the Secretary-General had received offers of troops from twenty-four countries. Italy agreed to lease Naples airport as a staging and collecting point. The United States Air Force in Europe flew Scandinavian troops to Naples, where they met Colombians who had come by air from Bogota and Indians who arrived from Agra in aircraft which started in Hawaii (this last journey of 8,500 miles was accomplished in twenty hours). Advance parties were gathered at Naples by November 10th and from there Swiss-Air undertook the further transport to Abu Suweir. Rations were rushed from American dumps in Europe. A few officers seconded from UNTSO reached Egypt on November 12th, the first units three days later; the latter could have arrived sooner, but Egyptian consent was needed (since Egypt was a victim of aggression and not a transgressor), and Mr. Hammarskjöld had to go to Cairo himself in order to negotiate the terms and conditions of their admittance to Egypt. By February 1957 the force had been

---

[1] Brazil, Canada, Ceylon, Colombia, India, Norway, Pakistan
[2] But there was an unofficial advisory council consisting of the ambassadors in Washington of the countries which were providing troops. This body was regularly consulted by the American administration which, especially during the truce negotiations, took no important action without reference to it.

built up to a total of 6,000 men and officers from ten countries. None was willing to lend its contingent for more than twelve months, and by the end of 1957, although contingents remained, their composition had completely changed and only General Burns himself and his staff officers had been in the area from the beginning.

The assembly of UNEF was a miracle of improvisation which would have been impossible without the long-distance telephone and the sleepless exertions of Mr. Hammarskjöld and a group of other international servants in New York during the first week of the crisis. The main lesson was that if the members of the U.N. wanted such operations to be undertaken, they should equip the organization with regular machinery before the next emergency occurred. The next major crisis was to be in the Congo, but in the interval the U.N. was invoked in Lebanon and Laos, and the rise of the Secretary-General, an inevitable concomitant of his role in the Suez war, began to arouse distrust in Moscow.

The U.N. Observer Group in Lebanon (UNOGIL) operated during the last six months of 1958. It was dispatched by the Security Council to watch the Lebanese frontiers and report on the truth or otherwise of allegations that insurgents in Lebanon were receiving Egyptian and Syrian help. Again the U.N. did what it could do with great promptitude. The day after the Security Council's instructions the Secretary-General transferred three officers from UNTSO to Beirut and a week later UNOGIL began to work as a fully constituted body. Its task was exceptionally difficult, because no more than one-eighteenth of Lebanon's frontier with the United Arab Republic was under the control of the Lebanese government and much of it was ill defined and in difficult country. At its peak UNOGIL numbered close on 600 military observers from twenty-one countries, equipped with 290 vehicles and patrolling at one time 8,500 miles a day. Besides mobile patrols the group had permanent observation posts, some light aircraft and helicopters, and an evaluation unit at its headquarters. It was accused in some places of producing erroneous intelligence and it was hampered in the middle of its operations by the landing of American forces at Beirut at the request of President Chamoun after the murder of King Feisal of Iraq in Baghdad, but whatever the true value of the information provided, there was no doubt of the need for information in a confused situation. UNOGIL acted as the eyes and ears of the Security Council and the main question when it was withdrawn in December 1958 was how to improve the Council's sight and hearing. Less than a year later, in September 1959, the Security Council established a U.N. presence in Laos in order to clarify a situation. The government of Laos having appealed to the U.N. to send forces to help it against an insurrection allegedly supported by Vietnamese Communists across the Laotian border, the Council appointed an inter-governmental committee of four to go and see. The creation of this committee on the model of the Balkan commissions rather than their more effective successors seems to have been opposed by Mr. Hammarskjöld, who subsequently sent a personal representative to Laos.

The Secretary-General's independent action in this affair may have fostered the Russian hostility to him which was to become open and vigorous during the Congo crisis. Appointed to his office in 1953, Mr. Hammarskjöld had conducted himself at first with a reserve and restraint which even a British civil servant might have envied, but Suez forced him to exchange his reticence for a leading diplomatic and executive role. After Suez he was quickly called upon to restore relations between Cambodia and Thailand, to extricate the Americans and the British from the Middle East in 1958, to deflate the Laotian situation and ultimately to tackle in the Congo a series of problems which nobody else was prepared to touch. Under his direction the U.N. was beginning to look a little bit like an independent power, or at any rate like an organization with a sense of purpose and a sense of direction. This flowering of the U.N. had been a consequence of the rise of the Secretary-General and was not in accord with the conception of an international organization subordinated to the several wills of the major powers. The fact that Mr. Hammarskjöld went out of his way to stress his prior obligations to the minor powers was no doubt further cause for irritation to such champions of a

nineteenth century order of things as Mr. Krushchev and
General de Gaulle. To them—and to the principal framers of
the Charter—U.N. action was action which followed agreement among the major powers, but now it seemed that the permanent officials in New York and the majority of the U.N.'s
newer and lesser members were losing sight of first principles.
Under the Charter the U.N.'s charge and its powers were (and
are) subordinate. Each of five members singled out for preference in 1945 was authorized to prevent initiatives by the Security Council of which they did not approve, with the result that
the U.N. could hardly intervene to keep the peace unless all the
permanent members of the Security Council wished it to do so
or did not bother to prevent it. When, as sometimes happened,
a different result ensued and the privilege of a permament
member was circumvented, that member had to consider how
loud and long his protest should be. The Congo operation
elicited a strong and sustained protest from the U.S.S.R.
which, after having voted in favour of the Security Council's
initial resolution, found the U.N. doing what it should not in
the Russian view do, and thereupon proclaimed in effect that
the powers of the U.N. had increased, were increasing and
ought to be diminished.

In the Congo the U.N. assumed a series of separate tasks. In
the first place it was invited to intervene in order to enforce the
departure of Belgian troops who had returned after the first
disorders and whose presence in the newly independent state
was interpreted as a threat to peace within the meaning of
chapter VII of the Charter. The U.N. consistently called for
the withdrawal of these Belgians and later of other foreigners.[1]
Secondly, the U.N. had to prevent the intrusion of the major
powers into the heart of Africa, bringing with them the cold
war and perhaps worse. Here the U.N. succeeded, and its success, if maintained, may turn out to be one of the two or three
decisive factors in the history of the immediate post-war period.
The U.N. succeeded further, to an astounding degree in the

[1] But not civilians. Helpful Belgians exist and, despite propaganda to the contrary, the U.N. has never attempted to remove
them.

circumstances, in keeping the Congolese economy going, providing elementary services, alleviating disease, preventing famine and protecting life. But it also found itself holding the ring in what amounted to a civil war between rival Congolese leaders, and it was forced to defend itself. For these two last functions it was ill prepared.

The necessity for U.N. intervention in the Congo was the breakdown of authority caused by the disintegration of the Force Publique, which fell to pieces either because of its inherent inadequacies (it had, for instance, no African officers and was badly paid) or, as has been alleged, because of the blandishments of rival Congolese leaders armed for this purpose with foreign gold. The result was a mixture of anarchy and warlordism and a grave threat to the peace of Africa and, if the major powers were forced or tempted to take a hand, eventually of the world. The Congo had celebrated its independence on the first three days of July and the mutiny of the Force Publique in Leopoldville occurred on July 8th. Other mutinies and outbreaks of violence followed and the Belgians sent paratroops to protect their citizens. The arrival of Belgian troops in Leopoldville on July 11th and their methods in some instances increased the rancour and the violence, and the situation was now so serious that the U.N. was immediately invoked and was asked to send a force to restore order.

The Security Council's crucial debate began on July 13th and the decision to intervene was taken in the early hours of the 14th. On that day the Secretary-General, who had already been making strenuous preparations, appointed the Swedish Major-General Von Horn, at that time Chief of Staff of UNTSO, to be Supreme Commander of the U.N. force and, again on the same day, arranged for eleven other officers, five field service men and five radio officers, all from UNTSO, to leave Jerusalem for the Congo. On the next day the first 600 U.N. troops reached the Congo from Ghana and Tunisia and others were standing by in the same two countries and in Morocco and Ethiopia. Food had been promised by the United States and Britain. Within four days of the Security Council's resolution 4,000 troops had been pledged to the operation and 3,500 of them had arrived. The figure rose to 8,000 on the 26th and 11,000 on the 31st. It went on growing during August and later reached nearly 20,000 from fourteen countries. In the first two weeks Kano airfield handled 950 flights, seven weeks' traffic at the normal rate. Combatant troops and police came from more than a dozen different countries, and yet others provided signals, supply, planning, ordnance, engineering and medical units, as well as aircrews, groundcrews and maintenance staff for the airlift. The staff work fell on an Indian brigadier and a British U.N. official, and the Secretary-General also had an advisory committee drawn from fifteen Afro-Asian states, Canada, Ireland and Sweden. The Belgian armed forces retired once more, evacuating all the Congo except Katanga by July 23rd; the U.N. force entered Katanga on August 12th. The U.N. had gone a long way to achieving its main purpose in less than a month.

But the achievements of the first four weeks were then undone. General Alexander and a handful of Ghanaians had persuaded the Force Publique in Leopoldville to lay down its arms; the Moroccans performed the same necessary task in Matadi and Thaisville and the Tunisians in Luluaborg; only in Stanleyville and Katanga were there still units capable of mischief. The U.N. had to create a new and reliable internal security force to give substance and reality to the Congolese Government, but although senior U.N. officials were well aware of this need they failed to fill it and acceded to Mr. Lumumba's demand to rearm the Force Publique. Sergeants and warrant officers were promoted to field and general rank, and far from sustaining the government the army took to indulging in civil crime with impunity. So no effective Congolese government could come into being and the continuing Katangan secession, about which the Force Publique in the rest of the Congo could do nothing, not only divided the Congo and ruined its finances but also led to dangerous quarrels and intrigues.

Mr. Hammarskjöld took the view that he had been instructed by the Security Council to get the Belgian forces out of the Congo but had not been instructed to use the U.N.

force to subject Katanga. The result was a quarrel between Mr. Hammarskjöld and Mr. Lumumba which arose out of a difference of opinion about the proper functions of the U.N. and was sharpened by Mr. Lumumba's suspicion that Mr. Hammarskjöld's refusal to use force against Mr. Tshombe in Katanga betokened a secret understanding with the Belgians. Mr. Hammarskjöld was, in fact, in an almost impossible position, because he was required to keep order but not interfere in Congolese politics and it was practically impossible to do the one without becoming involved in the other. His force had been sent to the Congo to keep order, but in the absence of a Congolese government a different kind of force and a different set of instructions were needed. Nobody was prepared to face this awkward development, and since the operation and the situation had become incongruous dispute was inevitable. Moreover, the dispute spread. President Kasavubu and Mr. Lumumba fell out, and their disagreement caused discord among outside African states and then served as a pretext for an attack on the U.N. by the Russians who, seeking to take advantage of dissension and to gain a foothold in Africa by winning the exclusive gratitude of Mr. Lumumba, accused the Secretary-General of being a tool of the colonial powers and intervened unilaterally with an airlift in support of Mr. Lumumba. The Africans, however, then rallied to the side of the Secretary-General, and Ceylon and Tunisia, with their approval (demonstrated by their subsequent vote in the Special Assembly), put forward a resolution in the Security Council in September which endorsed Mr. Hammarskjöld's attitude and insisted that intervention in the Congo should be undertaken by the U.N. only, the implication being a condemnation of unilateral intervention whether by the Belgians or the Russians or anyone else. When this resolution was vetoed by the Russians, the General Assembly was summoned to an emergency session under the Uniting For Peace resolution, and the Russians were again heavily defeated, being supported by no African state (except the Union of South Africa, which abstained on independent grounds).

The murder of Mr. Lumumba and the persistence of the

Katangan secession with foreign help gave events a sharp turn for the worse and the Security Council (some of whose members feared that President Kasavubu might turn to the U.S.S.R. and so give the Russians a second chance if the U.N. did not end the secession) repeated once more its demand for the withdrawal of Mr. Tshombe's Belgian and other foreign auxiliaries. On the first anniversary of Congolese independence chaos had been contained, outside powers had drawn away and a parliament representing virtually the whole territory was about to meet in Lovanium; violence had not ceased, but the number of deaths during the twelve months had been very much smaller than the toll of life in the Punjab in 1947, in Indonesia or Algeria or Angola. But this triumph on the part of Mr. Hammarskjöld and his principal lieutenants in New York and Africa was still endangered by the running sore of Katanga. Mr. Lumumba's successor, Mr. Gizenga, agreed to co-operate with other Congolese leaders, but only if Mr. Tshombe did too. The latter's fluctuations and prevarications eventually led the U.N. to use such force as might be necessary to evict Mr. Tshombe's foreign mercenaries and political advisers—a step which, if successful, was bound to lead to the collapse of Mr. Tshombe's régime.[1] But owing to delays imposed by diplomatic pressures and to inadequate air cover and some bad luck,[2] the operation failed and let loose a flood of anti-U.N. sentiment in the old colonial world. It also impaired the moral authority of the U.N. in a situation where moral authority sometimes had to do duty for —and did do duty for—efficient power. Shortly afterwards the Secretary-General was killed.

At this point there ensued a debate on the 'lessons' of the Congo. This salutary stocktaking was only beginning when these chapters were being written and it was still difficult in the autumn of 1961 to get the arguments into perspective, but we may make certain reflections drawn from the whole history of U.N. intervention since the war in the hope that they may serve

[1] After Mr. Hammarskjöld's death the Security Council instructed U Thant to do precisely this.
[2] Ethiopian aircraft under orders for the Congo were held up. A single aircraft on the other side played a decisive part.

as a point of departure for the more penetrating discussion that is undoubtedly required.

III

Intervention by the U.N. ranges from the inscription of an item on an agenda through resolutions to the actual despatch of a person or persons. The concept of the right to intervene has been cautiously extended at the talking end. At one time British representatives used to maintain that any discussion touching affairs in the Union of South Africa was in itself an infringement of article 2 (7) of the Charter, which prohibits intervention in the internal affairs of a sovereign state. In opposition to this view it was argued that it is impossible to decide on the legality of an issue without discussion, and it would seem that the more stringent view has at least ceased to be respectable. At the other end of the scale intervention by persons, as opposed to intervention by words, has taken various forms. Action is bound to vary because circumstances do not repeat themselves, but certain main types of intervention can be distinguished. There is first of all the mere presence of a U.N. body which is clearly incapable of using force for any purpose. The object of a mission of this kind is to get and publish information, so that antagonists may be inhibited (Kashmir, Jerusalem) and the world may judge what is going on and be the less likely to take misguided action. The need for intelligence has always been cardinal, but great events have often been set in train on the basis of ignorance and miscalculation; the interventions in Russia after the 1917 revolution provide a classic example. In Lebanon in 1958 and in Laos in 1959 the U.N. sought, on the whole successfully, to find facts and the result of its observations and findings was to deflate crises. A U.N. presence may also serve a useful purpose in keeping rival outsiders outside. The Congo could have become an international battlefield if no U.N. force had been interposed.

The second category of U.N. intervention is intervention in

force in order to hold a ring or police a border. Here Suez is the prime example. And thirdly there is active intervention such as we have seen, in very different forms, in Korea to resist aggression and in the Congo to oust armed foreigners and maintain law and services.

There are many limitations on the range of U.N. action. There is first the question of money. The U.N.'s annual budget is between $60 and $70 million and the Congo operation has been costing $8 million a month. These sums are absurdly small —the defence expenditure of the Nato and Warsaw Pact countries runs at about seven hundred and fifty times as much as the Congo expenditure—but members of the U.N. are unwilling to increase their regular subscriptions and sometimes refuse to contribute anything at all to a special operation. At present countries which provide troops and other units in an emergency pay normal (i.e. home) salaries and provide the equipment, and the U.N. has to raise a special levy to meet the rest of the expense. It has been suggested that all members should contribute to a special fund to be earmarked for emergency peace-keeping operations, but it is doubtful whether many of them would agree to pay in advance with their eyes closed what they now refuse to pay when they can at least see where the money is going. On the other hand, a special fund has an air of temporariness which may make it easier to raise money from governments which are willing to make some contribution to peace-keeping operations but recoil from subscribing to anything too explicitly permanent. Those who argue against a special fund and in favour of a more regular contribution complain that a special fund sanctifies a false principle in that the peace-keeping functions of the U.N. ought not to be regarded as an abnormal activity. They are on the contrary among its general purposes and should therefore be a charge on its regular budget. (The expenses of the smaller observation and investigation tasks are already met in this way.) But the ordinary budget would have to be trebled. The problem, it must be emphasized, is not a financial one. Governments can easily find the sums involved if they wish to, for they have only to get people to contribute the cost of one cigarette a year to keeping the peace. The

problem is one of political will, of the attitude of governments
to the U.N. At present the U.N. staggers along financially with
a real danger of complete collapse, tempered by the thought
in many minds that if the worst came to the worst the United
States would pay. But the United States already pays a high
proportion of the bill, and even if it were willing to pay more,
one effect would be to enfeeble the U.N. in another way by
laying it open to the charge of piping to the American tune. At a
time when the Russians are attacking the U.N. it is most inexpedient to increase its financial dependence on the United States.

Secondly, there are constitutional and legal difficulties. The
U.N. is subordinated to the wills of its more powerful members,
and the Russians at least have consistently opposed every attempt to depart from the letter of the Charter, however much
they may have played ducks and drakes with it. Nor is the
U.N. entitled to intervene in any country unless it is acting
under chapter VII of the Charter (in which case article 2 (7)
does not apply) or is invited by the government of the country
to do so (in which case, as Suez showed, the inviting country
will lay down conditions and may take its time in discussing
terms). If there is no effective government, then presumably
the U.N. could dispense with an invitation, but confronted with
an unwilling government, the U.N. can do no more than seek a
more willing host across the frontier. Nor does an invitation in-
variably provide an adequate legal basis for intervention. An
invitation to intervene may be legally improper, for a government is not entitled to seek outside support in a civil war; such
an act is repugnant to the view that the people of a country
have the right to determine the nature of their government.
This doctrine has been acknowledged on a number of recent
occasions. It was an essential part of the case for American and
British intervention in the Levant in July 1958 that the governments calling for help were threatened by external and not
internal enemies, and in the Korean war the Russians used the
argument that the conflict was a civil war in order to deny the
legality of the U.N.'s intervention.

Next we come to political hazards, which can be summed up
in two questions: Will the Russians ever allow another opera-

tion like the Congo expedition to be mounted again? Will a
group of local states combine to keep the U.N. out and run a
show themselves? The extent of the rebuff suffered by the
U.S.S.R. in the Congo has never been fully appreciated, least
of all in Nato countries where Russian claims to be scoring off
the West in Africa are taken at their face value and even magni-
fied by loose talk about successful Communist conspiracies. In
the Congo the Russians, flouting African nationalism and apparently forgetting that Russian faces are as white as Belgian
ones, intervened unilaterally and ran an expedition of their
own which failed. The political miscalculation and the subsequent humilation were severe, and the Russians may use the
veto to prevent the recurrence of a situation in which they
might again wish to intervene unilaterally but would be unwilling to risk another such repulse. The veto, however, has not
proved as reliable as it seemed to be before the Assembly devised ways of circumventing the Security Council.

The counterpart to the veto in the Security Council is a
majority in the General Assembly sufficient to block action in
that body too. Any power wishing to inhibit the U.N. may do
so by collecting enough members' votes to stop anything happening or reverse a decision already taken. In the Congo the
Russians may have intended to conjure up an African group
which would split with the U.N. over the question of supporting
Mr. Lumumba against his rivals. Nor was such a hope mere
moonshine. Many Africans were deeply hostile to Mr. Hammarskjöld on this issue. Thanks, however, mainly to President
Nkrumah's second thoughts,[1] they did not carry their opposition to the point of wrecking the U.N.'s mission. If at one time
the talk of an African High Command seemed directed to gaining exclusive control of African affairs for a pan-African group,
such ambitions were countered by African confidence in the
Secretary-General personally and by the revelation to Africans
of their own divisions. In Africa therefore the first steps have
been in the right direction, and as Congo-like troubles spread
southwards to Angola, Mozambique and South West Africa,

[1] He began by supporting the final communiqué of the Casablanca conference, which pointed the other way.

there is at least the hope that the African impact on events will be made within and in support of the U.N. and not outside it. If it is not, the chaos in Africa will be infinitely worse than anything that Europe ever experienced during its own times of troubles.

Politically the U.N. is also inhibited in special circumstances and in special areas. There are cases in which U.N. action is so dangerous as to be all but inconceivable. The outstanding example is a conflict which ranges blacks against whites. The U.N. could hardly intervene in such a quarrel without running a grave risk of destroying itself. Further, where major powers feel that vital interests are at stake (the Russians in Hungary, the Americans in Cuba) nobody will be allowed to intervene and the power concerned will itself intervene unilaterally. It is also supposed that the balance of power in the world makes U.N. action impossible in certain areas—Europe, North America, perhaps also Latin America—and it is certainly true that the most likely areas for U.N. intervention are Africa and the Middle East, since the local countries are comparatively weak and the major powers are scared of upheavals and anxious to see that nothing much happens there. The U.N.'s most likely field of action is one in which the major powers' main concern is to cauterize rather than inflame, and this attitude prevails where the major powers are anxious to find a quick solution to a problem without much caring what the solution is for the time being.

Finally, there is a different kind of political obstacle. Like any multiple organization, the U.N. suffers from an uncertainty of political will which inhibits action and leads to dispute when action is taken. In theory the Security Council or the General Assembly tells the Secretary-General what to do. In practice these instructions are too vague or general to be applied without further interpretation. This interpretation has in the past fallen to the Secretary-General, who was in effect required to fill a gap between resolution and action. Such a burden on one man is too great and endangers the whole system of collective responsibility by offloading too much of the responsibility from the collectivity on to an individual. In the Congo, for instance, the Secretary-General was authorized to use force, but in circumstances and for purposes that were inadequately defined. Some means must be devised—perhaps an extension of the Advisory Committee—to spread the political responsibility without derogating from the Secretary-General's paramount position within the Secretariat.

But when all these things are said and all these obstacles to action have been reviewed the fact remains that the U.N. has intervened in the past and is likely to do so again—unless prevented by sheer material deficiencies. The greater members have their privileges and a certain unwillingness to allow collective intervention in areas of special sensibility in the cold war, but it would be wrong to conclude that they can turn U.N. operations on and off as they choose. The fiasco of American intervention in Cuba may paradoxically facilitate U.N. intervention in Latin America, since Washington may be specially anxious to avoid any appearance of a second unilateral venture of that kind. And it is not without significance that the U.N.'s Congo operations went on even when the Russians were bitterly attacking Mr. Hammarskjöld and from the other side Mr. Rayeshwar Dayal, who was carrying out Mr. Hammarskjöld's policies, was being criticized just as bitterly if not so publicly.[1] Financial, constitutional, legal and political obstacles may all be surmounted in a particular case. But there are still forbidding practical difficulties. For the Congo the U.N. collected troops which turned out to be excellent; their discipline was remarkable by any standards[2] and their behaviour in requisitioned quarters would have astonished many Europeans who have had grievous experience of the passage of alien forces. But if another emergency were to arise tomorrow the Secretary-General would not know whether he could assemble a force or not, nor how long he could keep it in the field. This is the cardinal fault and until it is remedied peace will be ruled by coincidence.

[1] The Lebanon operation in 1958 was also carried on despite a Russian attempt to stop it. The Russians changed their minds and tried to stop the operation after it had begun, but they failed because a veto in the Security Council on one resolution does not rescind an earlier resolution.

[2] Except in one case when units which had performed their task were left too long with too little to do.

At present the U.N. is dependent on countries great and small for the launching of any operation except a minor observation task. However large the majority in favour of despatching a U.N. force, no action will follow unless the U.N. can borrow enough transport aircraft, and it is almost true to say that this requirement alone gives the United States a veto undreamt of by the framers of the Charter. Even a less powerful state like India can be all but indispensable, for the Indian army is the only army in the world which is both large enough to supply a whole range of combat and service units without being gutted and is also accepted as uncommitted in the cold war. Smaller states have to be wooed too. Their contributions to a force are essential if the cold war protagonists are ruled out (as they are at present), and although they have shown themselves willing to send troops abroad to keep the peace, they may be reluctant to allow their citizens to be killed in significant numbers in a distant quarrel. A democratic government might even be required to recall its troops at an awkward moment. This is not a reflection on the morale of the troops themselves (in the Congo losses and reverses did not impair military morale), but on that of civilians at home, who may become restive, especially if the conflict in which their relatives are engaged is obscure or seemingly trivial.

This dependence of the U.N. on member governments cannot be eliminated but it can be reduced, and if it is assumed that a majority of members will some time in the future wish to use the U.N. in emergency operations, it is clearly in their interest to do what they can in advance to make such operations smoother and more efficient than the frenzied improvisations of the past. One way of doing this would be to go back to the Charter, start again at the beginning with the Military Staff Committee and create a permanent U.N. force. There is no present prospect of anything of the kind. The larger powers dislike the idea of a force capable of being used in circumstances beyond their control,[1] and if they ever changed their minds

---

[1] Peoples may be less reluctant than governments. A poll in the United States in 1961 showed a considerable majority in favour of a permanent U.N. emergency force.

their smaller brethren would suspect them of wishing to create a new instrument with which to discipline lesser fry. From the U.N. point of view too a permanent force is at present undesirable and impracticable. Mr. Hammarskjöld himself argued against it on the ground that the circumstances in which it might be employed are too diverse and unpredictable: a permanent force would either turn out to be inappropriate to the next emergency, or it would have to be large enough and varied enough to cope with any emergency and thereby impossibly expensive. The U.N. will have, therefore, to continue to rely on forces made up of contingents contributed by members *ad hoc*, and the late Secretary-General laid down the principles that a U.N. force should contain no combat troops from permanent members of the Security Council; that it could enter no territory save with the consent of the government of that territory; that it should not fight except in self-defence; and that it should neither enforce a particular political solution nor influence a political balance decisive to such a situation. This framework cannot be taken too strictly and was in some respects overtaken by events soon after its formulation; it is elastic and may be expanded or contracted by resolutions of the Security Council or General Assembly in a particular emergency. But some such principles will delimit U.N. action in the next few years. Within them, and without raising a permanent force, the U.N.'s capacities can be appreciably strengthened.

Let us begin with the contingents of which a U.N. force is composed. The units offered to the U.N. in an emergency are not necessarily the units that it needs. Most countries offer infantry, which has only a limited usefulness in a police role unless it comes from countries like India or Malaya, whose forces have a high standard of personal discipline. In the Congo the small squads of riot police provided by Ghana and Nigeria (220 and 120 strong respectively) were worth several times as much as an equivalent force of African infantry. States which are willing to contribute to an international force have little idea in advance of what they can most usefully provide. Some states earmark units for secondment to the U.N. in a crisis—others are willing to do so[1]—but they receive no guidance on the training which these units ought to be receiving. Canada kept an infantry battalion available for U.N. purposes after 1956, duly innoculated against tropical diseases, but in 1960 it was asked for signallers. There is an equal ignorance at U.N. headquarters where, given a precise requirement at a particular moment, nobody is sure where to go to fill it.

The U.N. ought to have a small permanent staff at headquarters, a chief of staff who would make tours of inspection of likely national contingents, and a staff college. The U.N. could then work out a course of training suited to those contingencies with which it is most likely to be confronted. It would also develop a uniform staff procedure (the British is probably the most widely known in the world) and compile a document analogous to the 'Duties in aid of the Civil Power' which reposes in the safe at every British military headquarters—a document describing techniques for dealing with riots and using minimum force, prescribing exactly what units must bring with them when summoned, etc. This international headquarters would comprise an intelligence unit which could instantly provide information about terrain and climate in every part of the world (but not political intelligence). Gradually the staff college would create staff doctrines and a reserve of staff officers who had passed through its courses and returned to their own countries with some knowledge of how the U.N. works. The contingents too could be prepared for international operations if they were made available for use on non-political occasions such as the relief of distress in earthquakes and other natural calamities which involve relevant problems of organization, communication and transport, and also provide useful experience of going abroad and collaborating with units from other countries.

The U.N. cannot be expected to own much military material, but in one not very expensive respect it should be better equipped

---

[1] There are legal difficulties in many countries, e.g. Sweden, where conscripts cannot be made to serve abroad. Units from these countries have to be composed of volunteers unless the laws are changed.

than it is. Communications are crucial and mobile communications teams (similar to the G.H.Q. Reconnaissance Regiment developed by the British during the second World War) should be continuously available under U.N. control and trained to work in more than one language. There have at times been suggestions for providing the U.N. with a fleet of transport aircraft in order to reduce its dependence on the United States (the Congo operation would have been stillborn without the co-operation of the U.S. Military Air Transport Service and, to a lesser extent, Sabena), but the cost of acquiring and maintaining such a fleet is prohibitive.

The U.N. needs also a weapon of a less conventional and less lethal kind. All violent conflicts are today accompanied by verbal conflict, the latter being in fact more continuous than the former. Statements true and false can be broadcast with great speed; rumour and propaganda have become prime factors in the escalation of a dispute, and the nailing of lies and the dissemination of accurate information about what is going on should no longer be regarded (as they too often are) as matters of secondary importance. If the U.N. were equipped with special communications teams, these could give out information as well as collect it. In addition the U.N. might have a broadcasting station (the Pope has). Events in Katanga in September 1961 showed how inadequately informed the world can be, and it is unfair to blame the ordinary reporter who, having flown several thousands of miles to a strange country, is expected to file a story an hour or two later. In the Congo the U.N. got on the air for local audiences as far as circumstances permitted, but it has not so far succeeded in presenting its case or the facts to a wider public.

We conclude with a problem of special delicacy. In recent years weapons have been invented which can win victories without killing anybody. Certain gases,[1] for instance, knock people out for several hours, during which a position can be secured and control established. If such a gas had been used in the attack on the post office at Elisabethville in September

[1] Sometimes, but incorrectly, called nerve gases. The nerve gases properly so called are peculiarly frightful and deadly.

1961 the U.N. would have won what it set out to win by methods similar to the use of hosepipes by the police. Since many members of the U.N. have inhibitions about seeing the U.N. killing people, the regular use of non-lethal weapons would make them readier to sanction U.N. operations and thereafter to support them without flinching. But there are wider issues. The use of these weapons may contravene the Geneva Convention of 1926 and they have in any case an ill repute; to develop chemical and psychological warfare is possibly to advance the day when not only the U.N. but also anybody's political police could have invincible might. The prospect of settling disputes without any killing is alluring, but the price may be too high.

These measures presuppose the use by the U.N. of force in certain circumstances. What circumstances? Is it possible to establish any guiding lines in advance? The Secretary-General will use force if he is told to (and if he can get it), but when is it prudent for the Security Council or the Assembly to give such instructions? Negatively it is easy to see that the too frequent use of force is unwise, both because the wherewithal will cease to be available and because the image of the U.N. will be changed for the worse; it may also be unwise to try to act against the wishes of a major power which has the capacity to thwart U.N. action either overtly or by the back door. There exist real differences of opinion about the use of force by the U.N., and there is therefore a need for further consideration, and if possible codification, of this problem, for otherwise the U.N. will be thrown into hesitation every time force has to be considered and will lose adherents every time it is used.

But without venturing into these realms there are, I have tried to argue, a number of practical, salutary and inexpensive steps which could be taken now to smooth and buttress the U.N.'s peace-keeping activities. The U.N. secretariat would like to see these steps taken and so would countless millions of peoples throughout the world. But the initiative lies neither with international civil servants nor with private citizens. The members and animators of the U.N. are governments. Unless they strengthen their organization nobody can. Who gives the lead?

Chapter 5

Conclusions

PEACE, in the sense of universal and permanent absence of war, is a vital aim but not a reasonable expectation. Those who limit their aims to the attainable should not concern themselves with peace in this sense, for it will elude them. Yet the aim is nevertheless vital, for the desire and pursuit of the ideal is one way of minimizing evil; the ideal is, if not a goal in sight, at least a compass. There is too much violence; the prospect contains more violence; and the violence becomes ever more violent. In his efforts to reduce and control violence man needs a vision of non-violence. There is, moreover, a different ideal which may be attainable—peace in the sense of a generally accepted world order which includes effective machinery for settling disputes by persuasion and arresting violence by counter-force.

In this study I have given special attention to some of the immediate problems posed by the multiplication of states and by the rudimentary nature of inter-state machinery for discovering what is going wrong in the world and stopping it, and I have tried to set this investigation in the context of the two major bedevilments—the cold war and the encounters of continents and civilizations on a worldwide scale—of which we reminded ourselves in the opening chapter. I have suggested some of the things which practical men could do to eliminate some of the causes of strife and to create compulsive machinery for arresting some of the outbreaks of strife which are nevertheless bound to occur. These precautions and previsions would, if adopted, be an extension of the sphere of international politics, a recognition that there are more things that states could and should do to each other and for each other. But the problems of peace are not just political problems of this kind, for even if there were neither cold war nor clashes between civilizations, and even if the richer peoples were to assuage the wants of the new states much more than they do, and even if the United Nations possessed effective means for stopping wars, there are still two jokers in our pack. First, the scheme of international politics is itself in flux and we must beware of assuming that it will go on working in the way it has worked so far; and secondly there is a strong revolutionary force at work in the world which is not basically international at all and can be affected only marginally by international politics and endeavours.

International politics is an activity conceived in terms of states, recognizable and recognized political entities which have hitherto been few in number and each directed by a small ruling nucleus. International politics consisted therefore of communications and accommodations between a manageable number of *élite* groups. The whole of this concept is now in question. We have already noted the increase in the number of countries which count as states and as such have become members of the United Nations. But this development may be only a passing phase. The state familiar to Europeans, a unit delimited by tongue, accident and natural barriers, is not necessarily going to be repeated all over the rest of the world. Even in Europe it has never been universal, for the nation state has co-existed with larger and more variegated empires, and now Western Europe is beginning a federal experiment which, protestations to the contrary notwithstanding, should logically lead to the demotion of its constituent nation states. The states of Latin America are mostly related rather than set apart by tongue, while many African states are phantoms of the past which have adopted the federal idea even before full independence. In the Middle East existing states are not borne up by any tradition, but represent formal conveniences temporarily carried over into a new age. There is a fission-fusion process at work. When fission is in the ascendant we get a host of small units whose quarrels may be dangerous; when fusion gains the day, the units are fewer, but they are also so large that they must be difficult to discipline.

Within the unit, whether great or small, a similar process can be observed. Power is sometimes concentrated, sometimes dispersed. Europe has experienced a long and gradual process of dispersion, until it seemed that its ruling *élites*, like African chiefs, had had their day. The advantages of dispersion are

cherished by democrats; the disadvantages are the attenuation
of authority and the complication of the decision-making process, and when these disadvantages are felt with special keen-
ness a new authoritarianism is likely to arise, as in fascist Europe
between the wars and in parts of Africa today. The pendulum
swings one way and the other; in the nature of things it does not
pause at the golden mean. We may try to reduce its arc of flight
and even to make it tarry unnaturally long at the centre, but for
the rest we have to be prepared to cope with the extremes of
either sort. If there were no problem in the world save the regu-
lation of relations between states, then a world of few states
each governed by a small ruling class would be the most convenient dispensation. Modern Europe—which was also for
a time the modern political world—approximated to this order
of things until the other day. But that order has gone and since
there are other problems besides the pattern of state relations, it
had to go. For Europeans in particular it is important neither
to bemoan a past which, albeit convenient while it lasted, was
hardly just or durable, nor to retain a view of the international
scene and of international mechanics which are too rigidly determined by that past.

The second joker in the pack is revolution. By this I do not
mean Communism. I mean the changes that are coming about
within a great many countries in the world because of conditions in those countries and not at the instigation of people or
forces outside them; and here I wish to insist on a proposition
which may appear paradoxical. International affairs are
affected at least as much by events which are not international
as by events which are; by events, that is, which proceed within
a state without directly or primarily impinging upon the relations between two or more states. The history of Europe in the
last 600 years—and Europe is an international unit, not a state
—is not essentially the chronicle of the wars and alliances between the different European states, but the presentation of the
progress of that vast and strenuous and still incomplete movement of popular assertion throughout the whole continent,
which stretches from the peasant revolts of the later Middle
Ages to the risings of 1789, 1848, and 1917, whereby John Ball

and John Hampden and the Friends of the Rights of Man have turned society from something that stood on a point to something that rests on a base. And so it is now with the rest of the world. We Europeans tend to think of Asia and Africa at mid-twentieth century as continents at the end of colonialism, but this is to commit the error of thinking of an area in terms of something outside it. Of course the end of colonialism is important, but equally of course it is at its end and therefore what is happening now must be something else. What remains is more significant than what has been taken away, the persistent force more important than the occasion. And what is happening now is a revolution comparable with the tide of Europe's last six turbulent centuries.

This revolution is partially concealed. The end of colonialism has not transferred power to revolutionaries of the kind that I have been talking about. Power passed, on the contrary, to two other groups, one of which at least claims to be revolutionary in a different way. In the penumbra of colonialism, which casts a long shadow behind, certain objectives have had a greater prominence than social justice or economic freedom; these objectives can be summed up as getting level with the West, and they produced therefore, temporarily, an outward-looking rather than an inward-looking frame of mind, an attention at this stage to international rather than internal affairs. There is first the blunt fact of national independence, which is the political aspect of the search for equality with outsiders. The economic aspect follows almost at once—modernization, the determination to get what the West has in steel and aircraft and other twentieth century power levers and status symbols. The leaders on both these fronts are revolutionaries in the sense that, on the political plane they are in revolt against alien rule, and on the economic plane they are making a technical revolution. They are often the same people and they come characteristically from the upper middle classes.

A third aspect of this first post-colonial revulsion may be called the administrative. Again it arises out of comparisons with the West, for it has its roots in the feelings of shame with which the new men observe the corruption and inefficiency which often follow the change of régime. This feeling tends to be particularly strong in the officer class and so to produce *coups* which, officers being trained as they are, have a strong right wing element in them; but their movements are none the less reformist. Finally, there is the desire for cultural equality with the West, the assertion of traditions and beliefs which have been overlaid or even attacked by the colonial authorities and which the newly independent countries wish to see restored and acknowledged. Such feelings have contributed to the strength of traditionalist Muslim parties in the Maghreb and other parts of the Arab world, and also to the revival of Buddhism in Ceylon and its swollen political importance there. The leaders of this aspect of the revolution against the West are often reactionary in either the neutral or the bad sense of that epithet.

This revolution is by its nature transient and I have dwelt upon it in order to stress the likelihood that its leadership will also be transient. In some places these leaders are aristocrats, semi-Western in education and often speaking a foreign language by preference (Turkish in Arab lands a generation ago and French in the East today), who represent little but themselves and whose tenure of power has been prolonged by cold war policies. Less unrepresentative are the upper middle class politicians, nationalist and socialist as a rule (as these words have to be understood in that context) and in external affairs neutralist by contrast with the aristocrats among their neighbours, who tend to have a vested interest in alignment since they lack popular support and have to seek abroad what they cannot get at home. But however these new rulers may differ among themselves, few of them belong to the internal revolution of the future as well as to the national revolution of the past.

This internal revolution is not directed against the West. As it develops, it must be directed against the new rulers. It is, moreover, essentially Western (although it is unaware of the parallel), because it seeks what Western revolutionaries have fought for and won in fair measure already. Its natural leaders are in the lower, not the upper, middle class—among clerks and better off peasants, or postmen (Nasser is the son of a postman) and sergeant-majors, men who have been educated up to the age of about 16 and are anything but Communist. Such people have power in Asia already today because electorally they cannot be overlooked. The spread of communications and literacy has given them political influence and also, since politics now affects them by giving them or not giving them a school or a road, political views. A politician who has their suffrage is unbeatable, provided he keeps thinking about his constituents and not, as he used to do, about his principles. And what goes for Asia will soon go for Africa too. The underlying force and the reputable aspirations of this lower middle class are factors as significant and probably as potent as a supervenient military autocracy in a Middle Eastern state or one-party rule in an African one; Cromwell's major-generals and Robespierre's terror proved to be steps, if false ones, on Europe's road to justice and freedom, and neither of these episodes lasted very long. The West will make a bad mistake if it pays more attention to the episodes than the trend.

The same process is at work in Latin America too. So far it has been slow, but the pace is accelerating. Although the Mexican revolution was the earliest of the major revolutions of the present century, its sequels have been postponed by the persistent power of the Roman Catholic Church and officer classes, but now Guatemala, Bolivia and Cuba have heaved, and a recent sociological survey of Colombia has significantly noted a shift from the pattern of *coups* and counter-*coups*, wherewith the ruling *élites* diversified the years 1948–57, to a new kind of unrest among the lower classes on the land and in the towns. Whereas the former has made the headlines in the past, the latter is making the history of the future just as surely as the *philosophes* of the Enlightenment and the demagogues of the Revolution have turned out to be more effective in the long run than the cardinals, dukes and generals at the courts of the Bourbons.[1]

[1] Spain itself, from whose post-Napoleonic conservatism the Latin-American states revolted in a spasm of liberalism, failed in the nineteenth century to progress at all, and then failed in the twentieth to move from the first kind of revolution to the second. The liberal leaders of the Republic probably underestimated its urgency, and in any case they were given too few years before the Civil War threw Spain back into the past.

Our interest in these circumstances is that new states should come through inevitable revolution without too much painful violence or lasting aberration into authoritarianism, Communist or other.

The West's persistent weakness is to appear to be hostile to what is going on in new states. In their first nationalist, socialist and neutralist phase certain anti-Western traits were inescapable and so probably was the Western reaction, but nationalism is fast losing its anti-colonialist and so anti-Western implications, neutralism is coming to be regarded as respectable and even useful, and even socialism can be accepted in the capitalist West when it is fully appreciated that in states where no personal saving is possible the only possible form of capitalism is state capitalism. In other words the xenophobia of new states need not continue to be specifically anti-Western. There is a change of mood inherent in the circumstances and the Russians have already felt its touch. So long as they needed to do no more than embarrass and weaken Western positions, their task was obvious and easy, but with the liquidation of these positions the Russians have found themselves face to face with nationalist neutrals, with whom (e.g. President Nasser) they have not found dealings smooth. It is now Moscow rather than Washington which is coming to find neutralism unacceptable, for although in theory Moscow will back any national liberation movement, it does so with a reservation and a handicap. The reservation is the implicit assumption that the national liberation movement is in motion towards the left, although in fact the leaders in new states belong to the middle classes, whose attachment to Communism is minimal and whose leftward march soon slows down. The handicap is the conflict with Peking arising out of Chinese opposition to alliances with any but Communist movements. The conduct of foreign affairs is becoming more complicated for the Russians.

If by contrast the West wishes to ease its international problems it has to clarify its aims. I do not believe this is very difficult, for although there are widely differing views in democratic countries about what is happening in the world and what ought to happen, it is nevertheless possible to postulate two governing

Western aims which, lunatic fringes apart, should command general assent. The first is to prevent the further export of Communism by force. The West maintains that people should be free to develop in their own way. If they freely choose Communism, they shall not be denied,[1] but if they do not so choose, they shall not be forced. This proposition may seem to some people too negative, but it has the considerable virtue of simplicity and the considerable asset of commanding almost universal assent throughout the non-Communist world.

The second aim for the West is to keep violence within bounds. Western civilization is both convulsed by an internal quarrel and faced with the need to understand other civilizations which hitherto have been studied only by its scholars. Violence is in these circumstances not only specially probable but also specially dangerous. To prevent or limit it is a crucial task. Again the aim may be criticized as too negative or static, but properly understood it is not a retreat into mere conservatism, for it is not tantamount to stopping all change or even to stopping all fighting. The West has initiated change in plenty all over the world and continues to regard certain changes as inevitable and desirable. There is within the West room for debate on the expedient pace of change, but this is a debate within an agreed framework which posits on the one hand more change and on the other the avoidance of undue destruction in the course of change. However difficult it may be to achieve such an aim, the aim itself is, like the first aim, easily intelligible and widely acceptable.

The advantage of a modest definition of aims is the wide agreement which results from keeping to the essential minimum. The disadvantage is that a certain number of people, who agree with the basic aims but want to go further, chafe against what they consider to be overtimidity.

The advantage is a great one. The West has accepted too facilely the view that the world is divided between three kinds of political animal: Western democrats, Communists and the non-aligned. This division obscures the fact that the Western

[1] President Kennedy said as much in his interview in November 1961 with Mr. Alexei Adzhubei, the editor of *Izvestia*.

democrats and the great majority of the non-aligned are at one in wishing to keep peace, extend justice and honour, and forward the basic aims of the U.N. Charter. In his address to the General Assembly in September 1961 President Kennedy spoke of those who want to strengthen world order and those who do not. This is a fair antithesis, and so long as the West does not multiply its aims *praeter necessitatem* it is establishing a wide area of agreement in the world and pointing unambigously along a way that a vast majority wishes to follow.

The advantage is outward looking. It unites the West with other civilizations. The disadvantage, on the other hand, is domestic; it leads to debate, division and some malaise within the West, especially in the United States, where an uneasy spirit sometimes stirs, whispering that Americans are just as revolutionary as Russians. It is not at all clear whether the United States is a territorial state on the old European pattern or a political organ dedicated, like the U.S.S.R., to an idea. The last quivers of the revolt from Europe have not yet subsided, and a people which asserted its identity less than two centuries ago cannot easily reconcile itself to allowing its great enemy of today to steal all the admiration that is commonly given to the man who seems to stand for an idea and to have tomorrow on his side. There is an exciting generosity in the revolutionary impulse as well as a promise of violence, and it is hard to condemn the latter without seeming to have lost the feel for the former. So the heirs of the American revolution like to see themselves as the continuing protagonists of a revolution born of the Enlightenment, a movement to be contrasted with the later and less estimable revolution of which the Russians are the champions. Hence a picture of the West as a revolutionary force of a different kind, a polity in motion and dispensing living ideas. This picture seems to me not a faithful one, because it ignores as much as it reveals about Americans, and also because, though partly true of the Americans, it is not true at all about their Western allies.

For the past fifteen years American policies have been based essentially on a conception of the United States as a territorial state. Now, this basis may change, but there are few, if any, signs of such a change yet, and it is in any case important to distinguish between the image of a society and its impact. The impact of the United States on other countries is certainly revolutionary; in India, for example, American egalitarianism and the American lack of respect for intellectuals have proved far more upsetting than anything done by Russian technicians, and since the Americans are democrats they cannot help having a revolutionary impact on every hierarchical society with which they come into contact. But this revolutionary impact abroad does not give American society itself a revolutionary image. Americans wreak profound changes in other people's societies without seeming to these peoples to be revolutionary themselves. On the contrary they seem conservative, largely because they are rich. Consequently the desire to project the West as an alternative kind of revolution to Communism (quite apart from conceding that the U.S.S.R. is still revolutionary, which is at least an overstatement) is frustrated because it does not convince. It is an ill judged attempt, derived not from the facts of today but from dissatisfaction with those facts, to find a less defensive and less immediately restricted policy for the West and to seize some of the dynamism which has seemed to be the special attribute of Communism in world affairs.

And the West is not the same as the United States. At the end of the second World War the United States needed an alliance with Western European states and also to dissociate itself from the colonial taint which was attached to some of them. The alliance was formed, but to Asians and Africans it has had about it more of European colonialism than of American anti-colonialism. Therefore the image of the West as a whole has been counter-revolutionary rather than revolutionary, coloured by a European component resenting change rather than an American component in sympathy with it. Since the end of the war great changes, particularly material changes, have come about within European societies, but they have not on the whole shown themselves receptive to new ideas or good at producing them. The notion, attributed to a British Prime Minister, that Britain should stand to the United States as the Greeks once did to the less creative Romans is one of the century's hollowest forecasts. Britain and other leading European states have been playing a defensive game by ear, preoccupied with the solution of colonial problems to which they have addressed themselves with patchy skill but, understandably enough, little enthusiasm. It is difficult to get uplift out of lowering a flag.

The answers to many of the problems reviewed in this book are known to the West, however tentatively in some cases, but the West is incapable of implementing them because the Communist powers have, for the time being, different aims and answers. The converse is also true. The Russians have their view of the future world order, but they cannot achieve it because of Western opposition. Since the strategic balance of fear rules out unconditional military surrender and unconditional political surrender by either side, since in other words neither can get all it wants, nobody makes much progress in any direction. This is the curse of the cold war. Although cold war may easily become deadly war—the belief that nuclear stalemate and mutual deterrence are likely to prevent war seems to me comfortable rather than well found—few people act on this assumption; far more people are, knowingly or unknowingly, affected by the cold war's arresting grip on problems and patterns whose free play is thereby inhibited. One example must suffice.

We have been concerned in this study chiefly with major powers and new states and chiefly with their shortcomings: the limitations on the peace-keeping capacities of the former and the dangers to peace inherent in the circumstances of the latter. We have incidentally touched upon the activities of some members of another group of states: the fairly strong, moderately well provided and apparently uncommitted. The outstanding example is India, without whose co-operation no major expedition can at the present time be launched. Brazil may be, or about to become, another, and in Europe Sweden and Eire qualify. But one of the most terrifying things about the world today is that it is impossible to extend this list any further. The members of the class are neither numerous enough nor strong enough to enable any person of average perspicacity to sleep easily for more than half the nights in a year. Where can new recruits be found and how can they be trained and equipped? Is it sensible—to take a concrete example—for Britain to spend £1,700 million a year on defence if in an emergency it is not British forces but Irish that are used. How long will the middling states, by remaining committed in the cold war, remain also debarred from helping to keep the peace except in cases where they scent an immediate danger to their own security or their sacred cows? And how desirable is it in the context of the cold war to encourage a political disengagement by such states as Italy or Poland which might by such a shift add to the forces of peace, but only at the risk of upsetting the cold war balance and precipitating a bid for victory by the United States or the U.S.S.R.?

The weakness of the forces of peace is a reflection of the absorption of the middling powers (which have in this respect some of the virtues of the *bourgeoisie* in a national society) into the two great cold war camps, but since the world's political equilibrium depends in some degree on this very antithesis, any uncompensated defection from either camp brings with it a danger of war. The cold war freezes loyalties. It impedes the spread of neutralism in just those parts of the world where the most effectively neutral countries could be found. By the same token it increases the difficulty of preventing disorders elsewhere from developing into international affrays which, though their origins be different, could produce the same frightful consequences as a direct clash between American and Russian forces in Berlin or anywhere else along the lines of their confrontation. A great war can begin either at a point on this line or in a remoter spot. The end is the same, but there is a sharply irreconcilable clash between the safety measures required for the one and the other eventuality. Since the danger of war from a Berlin spark is commonly, perhaps correctly, judged more serious than the danger from a Congo fever, preventive measures against the latter are not allowed to interfere with the dispositions that have been taken to guard against the former. Neutralism is a bad word in the northern hemisphere. So the international order must get along with few neutrals in north-

ern latitudes, even though the more numerous tropical and
southern neutrals are barely able to undertake the tasks of
observing, policing, containing and suppressing the breaches
of international peace which are likely to occur in, and to
spread from, their parts of the world. But nothing is likely to
alter this situation except a change in the temperature of the
cold war itself.

There is no prescription for keeping the peace. The most that
anybody can do, whether he thinks or acts or does both, is to
try to influence men and events so that the balance may be
perpetually tilted to the side of peace (if on occasions only by a
hair) and the impact of accident or malevolence or stupidity
may be countered by built-in stabilizers and by an aware intelligence and a steady wisdom on the part of the principal
statesmen of the world and their advisers.

I would like in conclusion to summarize the arguments of
this study which are meant to be a contribution to keeping the
balance on the safe side. First, in relation to the major powers, I
have argued: that faced with disorder, actual or anticipated,
in another state, the basic question to be asked in deciding
whether or not to intervene is whether that disorder is likely to
get beyond the control of local government and threaten the
peace internationally; that although major powers have the
force and have used it in recent years to pacify and will use it
again in certain roughly definable circumstances, they are
increasingly reluctant to use it because they are afraid of pro-
voking a larger war, because they no longer have the ancient
conveniences of overseas bases, etc., and because the hostility of
the uncommitted world has become a sizeable deterrent; that if
major powers will only intervene in narrowly definable and increasingly rare cases, the guardianship of the peace is weakened
unless intervention comes from another quarter or an effective
alternative to force can be brought to bear to prevent or contain disorder. This reluctance of major powers to put forth their
strength is in itself no bad thing, since it gradually accustoms
people to collective intervention instead, but the growth of
collective action must keep pace with the decline in great power
action.

Secondly, while recognizing that new states may be as virtuous as older ones, I have argued that their relative weakness makes them less stable internally and that the pains of emergence all too often produce conditions peculiarly liable to engender disorder. Countering this instability is a major part of the human endeavour to keep the peace. It means aid by the richer to the poorer—aid in money lent or given, in men and women seconded for shorter or longer periods, in skills taught and habits imparted. In particular, since peace ultimately rests on force, I considered at some length the armies and police forces that these new states are acquiring. I have suggested that, with the help of Western technical aid in training, these forces should be made as efficient as possible in order that they may function with competence and rectitude and that if they are called upon (as they probably will be) to step outside their purely professional duties and run the state, they may be infused with the desire to do a job rather than do in an opponent.

Thirdly, the United Nations: the alternative to action by a great power is collective action by the United Nations (or possibly by a regional group). The provisions of the Charter for a Military Staff Committee and a permanent U.N. force came to nought, but in its earliest years the U.N. gained useful experience of observation and reporting on troubled frontiers. The Korean war was eccentric and therefore misleading, but out of the crisis of the fifties (Suez, Levant, Laos) the U.N. began to develop a capacity and a set of rules for intervention, culminating so far in its remarkably effective role in the Congo. But all U.N. operations have to be hastily improvised and no more than one operation of any extent can be mounted at a time. While there is no present prospect of equipping the U.N. with a permanent force, there is much that could be done (without altering the Charter) to make collective intervention more systematic and less haphazard. It is up to individual members to initiate improvements, since the U.N. is only the sum of its members; its will and its potency are alike derived and not inherent.

There was a time when it was almost true to say—and frequently said—that Britain was the world's policeman, but